ABOUT GRIEF

How to Cope with the Pain of Loss

EMILY ROWE

Every effort has been made to trace copyright holders and obtain their permissions for the use of copyright material. The publisher apologises for any errors and omissions and would be grateful if notified of any corrections that should be incorporated in future reprints or editions of this book.

The author gratefully acknowledges permission to quote Mary Schmich from *Always Wear Sunscreen*. Copyright © 1997 Chicago Tribune

Man's Search for Meaning by Viktor E. Frankl Copyright © 1959, 1962, 1984, 1992 by Viktor E. Frankl Reprinted with permission from Beacon Press, Boston Massachusetts

The cover artwork is an image of a sculpture called *Time Running Away* by Matthew Carney Copyright © 2009

I acknowledge this book was written on the traditional Country of the Bundjalung people who have occupied and cared for the lands, waters, and their inhabitants for thousands of years. We pay our respects to them as the Traditional Custodians and to Elders past, present and emerging.

All rights reserved by the author, Emily Rowe
ISBN: 978-0-6456728-0-0

To Matt. Still miss you every day. So grateful for our love. And Calpurnia. Teaching me daily what matters most.

About the Author

Emily Rowe is a grief and trauma counsellor, therapist and coach in private practice in Australia.

She has a bachelor's degree in Counselling and Psychotherapy, and another in Literature and History.

Emily offers both one on one, and group therapy online for grieving people looking for support while learning to live in a forever changed world.

You can find her online at http//: www.goodgriefcoach.net

When she's not working you'll find her hanging out with Calpurnia in the garden, the kitchen or at the beach.

TESTIMONIALS

"After the death of my father, I fell into a very black hole and didn't know where to turn or who to speak to. I knew Emily through social media and asked if there was anything she could do? Over the subsequent nine weeks of conversations and modules l was able to address the grief and associated feelings extending back to my childhood and began piecing my life back together. She provided me with an essential set of recovery tools and did so with great empathy and understanding. I would highly recommend her services to anyone who needs to tackle serious issues."

M.K.

"I first met Emily online and I was attracted to what she had to say about life and its travails. I was reluctant to get 'engaged' in my grief and Emily waited for me on this path until pain made me ready. Her course wraps around you and Emily protects you as you go. I have now rethought my grief and my way of being and healing; I see it as an expansion of the positive, joyful self, despite loss and pain. I have a much better understanding of the tools for true healing and one of Emily's great skills is to make sure you understand that love never really leaves."

L.M.

"I discovered Emily through her social media presence. I was 3 years into treatment for cancer and trying (unsuccessfully) to cope with the anxiety and isolation around COVID. Working with Emily has given me perspectives and skills that I practice daily- sometimes hourly to work through tough times. Her compassion, humor and laser beam insights are creating the change I've been seeking. I am so thankful to have found her. Emily is a gem."

M.G.

"I have been working with Emily for a few months now addressing some of the issues that arose over the loss of a parent under quite traumatic conditions. Emily has supported me in identifying my issues and working through them. I have appreciated her work with me, and even at inconvenient times (for her) she has been there and supported me with the immediate crises that have arisen. Her approach is honest and caring, the materials she uses are very practical. I value the insight that she has given me, along with her support. Thank you Emily."

I.R.

"Today I was sitting at my laptop, and I had an urge to write to you. Not for any pressing reason other than to just send a message of thanks, so here I am. Thank you. Thank you for being there for me during the worst phase of my life. Thank you for helping me feel a little less alone in the shipwreck that has been my life. Thank you for guiding me back to myself when I lost my way to do so. Just thank you."

A.T.

"I have found Emily to be the most responsive therapist I've worked with. Her unique style creates a person-person dynamic and is not hierarchical like traditional counsellors, that results in better communication, an openness, and less dependence on Emily as someone to 'tell you what to do' and more as a catalyst for self-assessment and accountability.

As I progressed through sessions with Emily, the growth and self-awareness were rapid, and we seamlessly transitioned from therapist-client to a coach-mentee dynamic. It's so hard to find a good counsellor/therapist to begin with, but to find and experience her unique and highly effective method that evolves with your progress was a real godsend."

H.S.

"I contacted Emily when a sudden unexpected devastating event derailed my coping processes. I have experienced considerable adversity and grief throughout my life but was knocked sideways by this event. Emily provided immediate coping resources and support and then a structured and supported process for moving forward. The process has been incredibly useful, and I am now quite a different person than I was 12 months ago. I frequently revisit the material and find even further growth and consolidation. Emily provides empathetic and professional support and coaching with humour and understanding. I can highly recommend Emily and her grief recovery services."

M.H.

"I first came across Emily's video about complicated grief shortly after my mother died. The concepts she expressed in that video prompted me to make an appointment.

During our first session, Emily gave me solid, constructive ways to mitigate some of the issues within the family that were coming to the surface after my mother's death. These helpful tools worked to keep things on an even keel emotionally for me during the memorial and during a time that I had been dreading for many years. As we worked together, I was able to clearly understand the dynamics surrounding family and my reactions to grief, and work through them positively with Emily's guidance.

Emily's approach is professional and supportive, and her own life experience brings a depth of personal warmth to her care for others. She patiently works through long standing deep issues, with excellent results. I highly recommend her book and courses to any who are navigating the rocky seas of grief and recovery."

M.S.

"I have had several experiences with psychologists over the years that have been helpful. Recently, when I was struggling with my relationship with my adult daughter, I was well and truly stuck. Working with Emily has provided profound insights and helped me develop the skills to better deal with the situation. Emily also focused on providing a framework for me going forward further empowering me. I am so glad I found Emily."

C.K.

CONTENTS

Introduction
Prologue
Before We Start

YOU

01. The Crucible - Processing Emotions
02. The Birdseye - Stretching The Story
03. Change, Choices, and Decisions

EVERYONE ELSE

04. Your Emotional Software
05. Manage the Moment
06. Choose Your Circle

CONNECTION

07. Different Kinds of Empathy
08. Degrees of Connection
09. Living Change and The Momentum Loop

Afterword
Reading List
Acknowledgments

Introduction

How To Cope with the Pain of Loss

"The real troubles in your life are apt to be things that never crossed your worried mind.
The kind that blindsides you at 4pm on some idle Tuesday."

Excerpt from "Always Wear Sunscreen" by Mary Schmich

Everyone will have a different blindside. For some it may be a death. Or an accident. A diagnosis. For others, a divorce, or a bad break-up.

What is the same in every blindside? It's that no one sees it coming. We all wander on through our days and hours and minutes and live with this assumption that it will just keep ticking over and we have control over our lives. That tomorrow will follow today, that we will pick up the dry cleaning on Tuesday and have a picnic on Sunday. When we are blindsided, we are challenged to still show up and play the game of life, even when we are feeling like we are not sure that we can.

In this manual I lay out quite simple ways to move into life that are intentional, considered, and safe. Eventually, in time, as you cultivate a relationship with uncertainty, you will be able to adapt to this new world order you are in. You will learn simple ways to grow trust in an unexpected future.

How to Use this Book

I encourage you to start at the beginning. It is designed to work through as a series of steps. The book is in three sections. Each of these sections has three chapters with recurring themes of emotions, stories, and change.

YOU

In the first section, You, we will explore what is coming up for you personally. How are you managing your heartbreak?

Your feelings at the moment are very distressing to experience.

In Chapter 1, The Crucible, there is a process where we explore what is happening to you. Just you. Your primary emotions are survival mechanisms that elicit specific behaviours. There is relief connecting the feelings to their purpose. That they have a greater meaning and can help you find a way forward.

In Chapter 2, The Birdseye, you will still the chatter. You will explore the nature of storytelling and the role it plays for people to make sense of their lives. Even in unexpected tragedies that make no sense there is a need for explanation. You will isolate the details of the event that has changed your life forever. When you connect to this point in time, the 'now' will help you focus and put the past in the past, and the future in the future.

When you reclaim your personal narrative, you let the rest fall away. This is important because your feelings align with the stories you are telling yourself. And often other people's version of things can be destabilising and feel threatening to your very identity.

In Chapter 3, Change, Choices and Decisions, you will study how people respond to change. Uncertainty creates wide and varied emotional reactions. Naming your emotional reactions will allow you to shift from reaction to response. You will focus on all the parts of your life that are challenged to change, and map how you will respond. Because we may live differently, but we all live in a day. You will learn how to cultivate acceptance of changes that you have no control over. And in doing so, the changes that you now must navigate will become clear to you.

EVERYONE ELSE

In Section 2, Everyone Else, the focus is on other people. How other people affect and influence how you approach your first principles (Emotions, Stories and Change).

In Chapter 4, Your Emotional Software, you will look at your meta-emotions. Meta-emotions are the feelings you have about expressing your feelings. Are you afraid to feel anger? Are you disgusted at your sadness? The modelling you received in your formative years as a child deeply affects your ability to articulate and express your emotions in healthy ways. I will explain all the variables that limit or strengthen your emotional literacy. Through learning about the impact of specific historical, cultural, and familial influences on your emotional expression, you can release all the baggage that isn't yours to carry.

In Chapter 5, Manage the Moment, you will learn of all the diverse ways people communicate. How people respond to your blindside reveals their ability to support you through the challenges you are facing now. You will learn to decode and depersonalise the different responses to your change of circumstances.

In Chapter 6, Choose Your Circle, we look for the key people. The specialists who can help you. Who can supply the knowledge you need? Who can help you to become better informed of potential outcomes for the choices and decisions you make?

CONNECTION

In Section 3, Connection, the focus is on how to function within a larger system of family, friends, and peers. How can you inform the people around you of what you need and how you need it? There are no guarantees people will be willing to provide it, but at the very least you have given those that want to care a roadmap of how to support you.

In Chapter 7, Different Kinds of Empathy, you will reflect on where you live emotionally within your community. Understanding how other people's behaviour is limited by their own personal skills can often make interaction easier. There are distinct kinds of empathy that humans offer each other. The interplay of expectations and the limitations that challenge our relationships when we are in crisis is significant.

You will learn the importance of boundaries when relating to people when you are vulnerable. Building healthy boundaries will alleviate a lot of secondary grief and abandonment created through misunderstanding.

In Chapter 8, Degrees of Connection, you will learn about the different modes of communication that people use, and how best to navigate them. The pyramid of communication illustrates how people choose certain modes of connecting. Technology can also become part of the message as people choose channels that distance them from your dilemma. You will learn tools that help you to direct the communication to the more meaningful exchanges you need or want. Having agency in this situation will empower you and alleviate feelings of abandonment and betrayal.

In Chapter 9, Living Change and The Momentum Loop, I introduce a powerful tool that will help you keep emotional balance and provide you with a way back to yourself. Not the self you lost in this moment of grief, but the self you always have been and always will be.

When you adopt these three different perspectives of you, everyone else, and where you connect, you will accelerate your understanding and uncover immediate answers to some perplexing relationships you may be in right now.

SHORTCUTS

There are quick fixes and insights you can apply straight away should you need them. If you are struggling to understand other people's behaviour, jump right in at Different Kinds of Empathy, Managing the Moment, or Degrees of Connection. If you are stuck in a problem-saturated story that is too dense to make sense of, then start at The Crucible or The Birdseye. If you are frozen and unable to see a way forward, start at Change or Choose Your Circle.

My desire is that this book stimulates a truthful and open dialogue about the lived experience of trauma and grief. The blindside. The interrupted present. The pattern breaks. The loss. The diagnosis. The estrangement. Whatever the tipping point of your sorrow might be.

I hope that people experiencing trauma and grief can take this guide to their therapist and use it as a framework for what they are experiencing. That I have articulated all the ugly truths of their struggle clearly for them. (Often ones that sufferers do not talk about for fear of being more isolated and alone.) This manual can provide therapists with insight into the actionable steps that a person can take to start to feel better and start feeling alive again.

If you love someone who is trapped in unprocessed trauma and grief read this book. It may be uncomfortable recognising your own limitations. When we can admit our failings, the sooner we can start to care more deeply and be honest about the effects of grief and loss. By reflecting on how to be and what to say, we step up. And when we feel confident stepping up, we do not let connections slide into silence and eventual estrangement.

When you are grieving and traumatised, it is difficult to process complex ideas. Your brain's response is to draw energy away from your executive function and keep you hyper-vigilant and safe. These are simple instructions distilled from complex ideas. This is purposeful design.

In the reading list, you will find the books I have read over many years that have informed this guide. There is a wealth of resources that I invite you to explore if you are curious to learn more.

And if you buy this for a friend, grab a copy for yourself too. It will change the way you think about your feelings, your stories and how to survive the untenable.

Prologue

"I was a victim of a series of accidents, as are we all."
Kurt Vonnegut - The Sirens of Titan

I was blindsided when my husband was killed on Thursday the 23rd of June 2011. Matt suffered a cardiac event and died on the living room floor at home.

He had been diagnosed with cancer only five weeks before he died. He dutifully received his treatment while being reassured that he was young, and the tumour was encapsulated. His illness was presented to us by the treating doctors as 'manageable'. His prognosis was good.

I never thought that the treatment would be what killed him.

His death came out of nowhere. Death does that though. It is one of life's painful realities. The never knowing.

It would be remiss to not admit that I had suffered loss before. There had been other traumas and tragedies I had endured. Each slowly robbing me of my sense of things. But none so much as to completely break my heart and destroy my sense of self.

One major trauma was watching the buildings fall to the ground from 16th street in Lower Manhattan on 9/11. On what had started as a typical crisp Autumn workday everything changed for so many. For those who died, their loved ones left behind. The trauma ripples beyond this event were global. Ask anyone where they were when the news broke, and they can tell you. No one has forgotten.

For many New Yorkers it triggered a stark re-evaluation of what their lives meant. As the smoke continued to hover over the city and the ink ran on the missing posters, there were a lot of big conversations occurring. If that had been the end, were people living the life they wanted? Or were they living a life they had fallen into? I realised that if I did not set intentions, I could very well end up alone forever. Over time I had fallen into the fever of the city. Sacrifice for success.

I decided that this was not the life I wanted. Within four months, after seven years in the city, I packed up and left. I had no firm idea of the future but armed with the deep knowledge that I was not living my best life; I struck out to find a new one.

I had packed up in Manhattan, the smoke still rising from Ground Zero and the city filled with fear and grief and found myself at the opposite end of the earth. Bruny Island, Tasmania. I went to see Matthew Carney, a sculptor I had met at SOFA in Chicago, just weeks after 9/11. The only landmark on Bruny Island as tall as a skyscraper was Fluted Cape. When I walked the track to the top of the Cape and squinted as I looked out to Antarctica, I imagined I could almost see the curve of the Earth culminating in its icy polar cap.

We drank red wine and talked until the early morning. As we played chess, we mourned this global catastrophe that had shaken the world order and everyone's sense of safety.

"We don't have much time," he said. And it turns out, we didn't. It felt like we never had enough time. In a morning, an afternoon, a day, or a week. He named one of his exhibitions "So Little Time," much to the laughter and derision of our fast-paced city friends who saw our creative life as indulgent and free from deadlines.

My PTSD became more pronounced. I was a textbook trauma sufferer. I had found my way to safety on the other side of the world and then the adrenaline stopped pumping. The energy ran out and I was stuck in a minefield of symptoms. I was safe, but still startling at a car backfiring. The smell of wood smoke from a neighbouring property sent me flying outside to see what was happening. Exhausted, I struggled to get out of bed in the morning after nightmares of watching those buildings fall. Haunted with hearing everyone collectively scream "No!" as we watched them collapse in clouds of dust and smoke, knowing thousands were being incinerated and falling to their deaths.

I knew I was unwell but was resistant to visiting a mental health care professional. The last time I had followed that path, (the earlier blindside of too many funerals for a twenty-five-year-old girl – thank you AIDS), I ended up medicated. Back then the pills worked. I stopped feeling depressed. But I was not feeling anything. I was the walking dead. So I weaned myself off the Prozac, and self-medicated regularly with weed and dirty vodka martinis. But post 9/11, no amount of weed or vodka was going to help me. My own prescribed treatment started failing.

Matt encouraged me to seek help. I was wary.

"Trauma is not character-building Emily. It is soul destroying. If you don't process what has happened to you, what has happened to you will shape you in unhealthy ways."

Only the son of a psychiatrist/psychotherapist could say this with such authority. Reluctantly, I agreed to see someone.

Surprisingly, Hobart was at the forefront of trauma treatment. In April 1996 there had been a terrible massacre. A mass shooting at Port Arthur where 35 people were killed and 23 were wounded.

My prerequisite for treatment was no pills. I saw a psychiatrist who was an EMDR specialist. EMDR, (Eye Movement Desensitisation and Reprocessing), is a time focused psychotherapy that enables people to access uncomfortable traumatic memories and process the connected emotions contextually. Now I will never know whether it was the EMDR or having the opportunity to offload what was churning around in my mind, or the combination of both, but I started to release some of the physical symptoms. The hyper-vigilance subsided. There was a little crack of light I could see that enabled me to feel the past in the past and the present in the present. Sometimes just admitting the struggles are real and you are having a normal response to a terrifying situation lightens the load a little.

Life calmed down. Matt and I got married. My business started getting some traction. We got pregnant. Halfway through the second trimester and I started experiencing extreme nerve pain from my shoulders to the tips of my fingers. I had been spending my days making intricate jewellery with tiny stones and silver wire. The doctor deduced I had carpal tunnel syndrome, and I was prescribed codeine and put in bilateral splints to manage the pain. My hands were numb, and they became useless, like flippers. I could not even open a jar.

April 30th, 2004, and I am having contractions. Our longed-for little girl Calpurnia was on her way. 5 am on May 1st she arrives - alert and singing. I am shocked back to wonder. This little miracle, this arrow into a shared future is finally here.

We head back to the cottage on Bruny Island and nestle into our new baby bliss. There is snow on the beach and the wind in the gums sounds like jet planes taking off. All around us the wildness reminds us of our good fortune. Cocooned in warmth and safety on the edge of nowhere.

Having Calpurnia is a huge vote for the future. My post-apocalyptic trauma fades away as I am showered daily in oxytocin. This amazing, beautiful creature rarely out of my embrace. Smiling and cooing and doing everything babies do. (Except sleeping). Each baby check-up she is hitting all the milestones, weight, eye contact, rolling over. When she decides to become mobile, she disregards crawling. Pulls herself upright with the table leg and hurtles headfirst across the room. At 10 months.

But no babbling. No words. When she is 12 months old, she has her first seizure. The doctor called it a 'febrile seizure'.

Her GP was calm about it. "Not unusual," he said.

But it proved to be the harbinger of a mystery that would be revealed years later. When I quizzed him about the language delay, he dismissed it. "She is young. She will catch up. It comes in at various stages."

But for Cal it did not.

She startled easily. Did not adapt to change. Did not interact with her peers at day care. At break time she would put classical music on, pull on her 'ballet' slippers and dance to her own reflection, a million miles from care. Finally, the bomb is dropped. My child and the words special needs are put in the same sentence by an educator.

This is a great unspoken blindside. Nobody goes into labour planning on having a special needs baby. And when educators flag your child, there are often other medical issues that manifest a different kind of trauma. Apart from the febrile seizures, an inability to sleep, and dragging her right foot when starting to walk, we had no idea what the future was going to hold. She was healthy. How can any mother complain if their child is still breathing? Any visit to a paediatric intensive care unit will teach you to be grateful.

We had moved to town by now and Cal's differences were more pronounced when measured up against her same age peers. The repetition compulsion was clear as she would spend hours watching the same DVD over and over. Her obsessive nature was evident with her endless fascination for shoes. Mostly other peoples. But she was smiley and happy and friendly provided she felt safe. Despite extremely limited language, she was far too socially adept to be diagnosed as autistic. So, we soldiered on.

A relative demanded to know 'what I had done to her', as 'she was born perfect'. It must have been my fault. I was to blame. There must be someone to blame. Another layer of trauma added with the weight of accusatory personal responsibility. My father, a paediatrician and geneticist, was far more circumspect. I cried on the phone to him, confused and overwhelmed.

"They want me to take her to OT and Speech Pathology and…" he cut me off. He had seen more than his fair share of children with unique needs.

"tell them to go to hell. You have just one childhood with her. Cal is Cal. You can spend it running around to treatments for delays that may correct over time and constantly reinforce for her she is flawed. Or just let her be who she is. You and

Matt are smart people. Do not hand her over to other people offering you promises with no guarantees. Just let her unfold."

He was right. I tried one course of speech pathology and Cal went from a struggling and rudimentary style of communication to none. She was smart enough to know she had been red flagged.

We settled into our new 'normal', but as any parent of a child with special needs will tell you, that works until you leave the front door of your familiar home. It is socially isolating, emotionally terrifying and time consuming. What a neurotypical child may learn in a week, may take your child 6 months. Or they may never learn it at all. So little time equals a lot less income. You have a lot less energy for anything else and a lot more anxiety about everything. You also experience a passive discrimination at the hands of other young parents who do not include your little family due to misunderstanding and ignorance around disabilities. Cal had a disability. It was not contagious. She was funny and sweet and kind. For all her struggles and vulnerability, her beautiful spirit shone. She radiated effortless pure love.

But I have returned to my trauma state. Those familiar neural pathways of hyper-vigilance, cortisol and distrust have lit up again. I am hit by a wave of despair. A lifetime of unprocessed grief catches up with me and starts altering the lens of my perception.

Life is starting to look extremely unfair. There is the grief of losing my young friends to AIDS, compounded by the grief of 9/11, compounded by this new reality. My child will not have the future I dreamed of for her. She will not attend a mainstream school. She will not learn to play an instrument, or drive a car or go to college, or move out of home. I do not know what will happen, but it's not what I expected. Another blindside. I fall to sleep every night worrying for her future.

Matt's sudden death broke me. I just wanted to fall apart. To disappear. To pixelate and vanish. And yet I didn't. I didn't because I couldn't. I was in this new world where I woke each morning to a huge absence. The person who had become my safety and my consistency, my true North was gone. The person who was always there to talk through difficulties and problem solve with was gone.

I was alone in all the responsibilities. I was alone as a parent, a provider, and consoler to my bereft seven-year-old girl. Her limited and hard-won vocabulary vanished, and she disappeared into a wall of silence, rage, and dissociation. This was not the plan.

On the afternoon he died I was at work. I was standing at the coffee machine loading it up to make another latte and I felt a seismic blast through my body. Every cell in my being became disconnected then recalibrated into something different. I knew this sensation. It was familiar. Ice cold fear. Terror.

I dropped the cup I was holding, and it smashed to pieces on the tiles. I turned to Meg and said, "Something is wrong. Something is terribly wrong."

Racing to the back room to grab my belongings I peel off my apron. I start crying as I head out the door – my boss and workmate looked at me like I have gone mad.

"Something's wrong." I told them. "Something is very, very wrong."

As I say wrong the screen on my phone lights up and its Cal's school. No nononono, please not Cal. Tell me Cal is ok.

I answer the phone and it is her teacher.

"Where's Matt? He hasn't picked Cal up. I've called and he's not picking up. Can you get her? We want to go home."

Why isn't he there? Why hasn't he picked her up? I look at the unanswered text messages and calls I've left on his number. I had been so busy I hadn't looked for a response. The last time I saw him, he was heading out the drive to go for his radiation. Day 15 of the chemo medication and he was ashen. Shuffling like an old man. He kissed me deeply at the door.

"I love you more than you'll ever know." he said.

I drove home on the phone – trying to piece together where he could be. The nurse at radiology confirmed he had attended his appointment. The treatment was brutal. Had he crashed the van on the way home? Maybe he had fallen asleep at home?

I called my neighbour.

"Stan – is the van there?"

It was.

"Can you check on Matt? He's not picking up."

I could hear his footsteps on the handheld as he approached the door. The knock. No answer. The callout.

"Matty?"

Checking the door handle. Hearing it turn.

"Matty?"

"I can't wake him up Em. He won't wake up"

"Call 000 – I'm on my way…"

I screamed at a God whose existence I'd long since rejected, as I drove like a madwoman over 100km an hour down that crazy road through the bush.

"Are you fucking serious?" I railed at God. I mean someone had to be in charge, right?

"Is this really how you are going to play this?"

I don't remember sleeping that night. The police had been and gone. The undertaker had been and gone and I was at my parents' house, with Calpurnia tucked up asleep, oblivious to what had happened only hours before. I remember downing large slugs of whiskey, chain-smoking and shivering. My neurotransmitters had been knocked sideways. Adrenaline, norepinephrine, cortisol. I didn't know whether I should punch someone, pass out or run away. But where to run away to?

There was no other place that Matt existed. Well, there was non-existence. But I had Calpurnia to care for. Non-existence, as comforting as it seemed, was not an option.

It took about six months before I was ready to talk about what was happening for me. And by then, everyone else had moved on. They didn't want to dwell on it. It wasn't 'healthy'.

I appeared to be coping. I hadn't killed myself. Yes. Really. The bar was set that low.

We can only ever see the world from our exact place in time and understanding. When you finally face your Alamo, your crisis that will tip you to the contemplation of non-existence you will utterly understand this. You will face the cold hard reality of your aloneness in the universe. Although you may believe that people who can support and understand you surround you, for many, your crisis will be their departure point.

And this will happen by degrees. The first to fall away will be the acquaintances, or newly formed friendships. Here, it is easy to withdraw and assume that the person who is suffering has people closer to them, that understand them better and you are getting in the way. Seems to make sense. It's a very pragmatic and convenient choice. You're off the hook. They will be the first people to stop calling and checking in – usually within weeks of the funeral. I forgave them. The Grim Reaper has cruised past and given them the finger. Reminded them of their mortality but didn't crash their car. Turns out they are just a random passer-by craning their neck as the ambulance arrives.

The next wave to crash out of your life will be the people you have known forever but you don't see that often. Their version of you, tucked away in memories of a past and a happy life of Christmas cards and occasional interstate catchups will simply cease to exist.

> You have become someone else.
> But who have you become?

Well, it depends on the day. Have you called me on the day after a nightmare? In my dream where my lips are pressed hard against Matt's, trying to force the breath of life up against the stale decay on his breath? I could not raise the dead. (CPR works in less than 12% of cases outside hospital settings but you wouldn't know this from how it is portrayed in films and on television.) Am I in another grief stricken round of perseveration where I am watching that day unfold in Robert Altman cinemascope? Trying to understand how a series of randomly connected snippets of a challenging day culminate in tragedy and death?

'I'm telling you this because it's spinning around in my head – whirring in my sloppy grey matter. This brain than can no longer believe that the world is a safe place. How can the world be a safe place when it has robbed me of my Matt?"

This is trauma. And most people cannot cope with it. I needed to find a way forward. To survive. To figure out what mattered to me now. What was important to me? My happiness was in the past and only existed in my head as memories that I was struggling to access. And when I did, they were too painful to visit. They just existed as another harsh reminder of what Calpurnia and I had lost and didn't believe we could find again.

Therapy was the next destination. It is where well-meaning and perplexed family or friends park you to get fixed. They imagine you will return and resume a 'normal' life. But what does a normal life look like now? There was no normal. I hardly felt alive. And the behaviour of the people around me compounded the initial trauma I was suffering, leaving me increasingly isolated.

My first therapist fired me. I think I was so traumatised that I traumatised her. She could not hold the space. Clearly her career had been one of handing tissues to the worried well. She simply did not have the tools for this level of immediate trauma.

I went to see George Klein. George knew how to hold the space.

"If we lived forever Emily, you could grieve 10,000 years for losing Matt and it would not be enough,"

And when I became self-conscious about my singular weekly outpourings of tears and whimpers, he would look at me evenly as I apologised.

"You come and we eat the sour pickles together Emily."

He showed me such expansive compassion, profound wisdom, and kindness that I will be eternally grateful for.

At the same time as I started seeing George, I received a scholarship to study counselling and psychotherapy. I was so confused by what was happening to me. The way people closest to me had responded to my trauma was baffling, and I was seeking any answers I could find.

I had dabbled in Rational Emotive Behaviour Therapy that was the forerunner to Cognitive Behavioural Therapy (CBT) when I was in New York. This was what had landed me on Prozac. In hindsight, it was the wrong kind of therapy for the first round of blindside. This was back in the early 1990's and there was little dialogue around trauma. It happened to soldiers and first responders, not young women who nursed their young friends with AIDS dying by degrees.

I needed to understand the perspectives, the tools, and the schools. How else was I going to heal? I exploded into George's small consulting room at the front of his house each Saturday afternoon with my head and heart both full of confusion.

I come from a large family with a very wide circle of friends. My late husband and I both had extended friendship circles and yet, I was completely isolated in my grief and loss. And it all felt like a personal rejection of me. Now, we all experience rejection in life. It hurts. But everyone? Was I really such a terrible person?

Together George and I uncovered that I had limited emotional literacy, poor boundaries and was still working from pure survival instincts. I was barely able to decide what to cook for dinner. (We ate a lot of 2-minute noodles.) It is hard to see past what is happening for you when you are traumatised. Your prefrontal cortex is not functioning well in the state you are in. I would feel nauseous and sweat just getting into the car to drive. Everything seemed so difficult. It was impossible to connect thoughts clearly.

Over time I started to understand what was going on. It didn't make it easier. Each upgrade of knowledge was a letting go of earlier understanding. And another life. I was changing. I was not only traumatised and grieving the loss of my husband. I was grieving the loss of myself. The person I was in that relationship, defined by that life and the choices I had made up until now had died as well. I had lost my witness.

When you lose the person you love, you lose a witness. You lose that person who mirrors back to you who you are in all your moments. They are the one who sees you grapple with the complexity of a creative challenge you are facing. They are the one who knows what you like to cook, what you like to eat. They are the one who watches your interactions with others. Who shares your reflections and concerns about relationships you are finding strained, or complicated. They are the one who knows how little/much sleep you have had in the night if your child has been restless. They are the one who you have shared parts of your story with that no one else knows. They can see the way you care. How you try and include people who are isolated and abandoned. They are the one who tells you not to worry but also relaxes in the knowledge you've got that covered. They have seen you at your best. They have seen you at your worst. Together you speak volumes in a space fraught with silence and small muscle movements.

This you. This person who is alive in the presence of this love, where do you go when your witness dies? You have outsourced this sense of self to be defined by this watchful loving gaze of your witness and now? No one sees you anymore. Not like that.

When you lose the person you love, the person you were with them dies too. You are no longer that person and flail around the edges of this diminished identity until you're ready to let go.

You must become someone else. The person who survived losing the safety of your witness. It isn't easy. And transitioning your love story to 'then', to the past, hurts like hell. You must push away all that sentimental reminiscing to recalibrate yourself into a full person again. One that can say that was 'now'. And this is 'then'. I was frozen in the 'And then'. What was going to happen next? The pattern interruption of a full and engaged life is like nothing else. All roads lead to then.

I was tired. Remember one of my first blindsides? 9/11 and I made a massive 180-degree turn. I had made new choices!

New decisions! I had laid a bet that aligned with my principles and values. Downsized from a fancy cashed up city reality for the pastoral life of love, nurturing, and creativity. Here I was, 42 years old and I was going to have to figure it all out again?

College was the best place for me. It provided me with specific readings, tutorials, and assignments with a defined goal of passing and becoming a qualified counsellor. Learning about all the different schools of therapy allowed me a thorough overview of the way different therapists, philosophers and sociologists have approached human struggles.

I am writing this prologue in 2022. In 2020, as the global pandemic erupted, I imagined the webs of interconnected people who have suffered their own blindsides and what it will take to process the collective trauma we have all experienced. We are all grieving the loss of friends and family. Of a way of life pre-COVID-19 that seems like a carefree dream.

August 2020, my girl Calpurnia finally received her elusive diagnosis. She has a rare genetic syndrome called Beta-propeller Protein Associated Neurodegeneration. (BPAN). It isn't carried by either parent. It is a spontaneous mutation that occurs at conception. Less than 500 people globally have been diagnosed with BPAN. How unlucky would you have to be?

This latest blindside has been rough. There is no cure for her condition. Sometime in her late teens or early adulthood she will develop dementia because of the iron deposits building in her brain. She's almost 19 and the clock is ticking.

All those hard-won skills she will lose one by one until she will no longer talk, walk, or understand much of the world she is living in. She will eventually lose the ability to swallow and need to be tube fed.

She does not understand what her genetic syndrome is. What her future looks like. Time is some ridiculous idea to her, and most things happen at 4pm on a Tuesday if you ask her. Her understanding is uncomplicated by time. But I know. Every day I work with this new anticipatory grief. I explore all the complex emotions as they come up. I unravel all the narratives around the fact of her illness. I embrace every single moment I share with her while she is still well. I can't change what has happened. I can't fix that 'spelling mistake' on gene WDR45. But I can change my perception of things. I can define my values and live according to them in a way that keeps me resilient, trustful, and joyous. Holding on lightly to this moment now.

When we have suffered loss, we never reach closure. It doesn't ever end. How do we keep our humanity in the face of terrible circumstances? How do we keep caring beyond events that break our hearts? It's not easy, but it is possible. And I am going to show you how.

Before We Start

What you think, and how you feel, will affect you physically, and how you treat your body will also affect how you think and how you feel. You are embodied, and how you treat your body, will affect your ability to achieve any kind of balance after a loss.

When you are vulnerable, there is a hope, even an expectation that others will care for you. This idea is from times when we lived more communally. Earlier generations lived in larger households, closer to extended family, with connections through community affiliations and churches. Today we are living in a loneliness pandemic. People are living alone, with no community of care to help them in their day-to-day life. This is disastrous for the most vulnerable in our communities. And while you are grieving, you are one of the most vulnerable.

Getting through the everyday tasks that you previously did without even thinking about has become more difficult. If you have a person, or people around you that can care for you, you are incredibly lucky. Most people are stretched to their very limit with their own lives and are unable to create time to help you in your time of need. Maybe you were the person unable to do it for someone else in their time of need.

It is easy to feel angry and distressed when you are neglected in your time of need. This will not help you though. Acknowledge it, then park it and step into a response that will be beneficial to you. Commit to your self-care. Take responsibility for your basic needs. This is a really challenging time in your life and being able to care for yourself and creating some positive habits, is going to support you right now when you need it most.

In this chapter, we are going to look at the physical effects of trauma and what you can do to give yourself the best chance to feel better. I understand at this point it may seem easier to hide in thought or feelings. Our physical reality feels quite detached. This is also part of your trauma response. Your body can feel either so wired, or so numb that you forget to eat, or sleep, or exercise.

Do you have any physical or mental conditions that you were managing before the loss? If so, make sure that you continue to seek support and treatment for these. Grieving is so hard on the body and the mind; any pre-existing conditions will be affected by trauma.

Let's first take stock of where you are at right now. Answering these questions and evaluating your state will help you generate the responses you need to care for yourself. For some, this may be a foreign idea as attending to yourself is not something you have reflected on before. Right now, your well-being depends on it.

What Does Trauma Feel Like?

You are probably feeling all over the place at the moment and you are wondering what is happening to you. What you are experiencing is a trauma response. When you have suffered a loss, you often live in fight or flight mode with a shaky nervous system.

There are many different trauma symptoms. You might experience all of them. You might only experience a couple of them. The effects can range on a spectrum of intensity from mild to severe symptoms. Your responses may also not be specifically related to a trigger such as a thought or a real time event and sometimes may seem to come out of nowhere. This is normal.

Basics of the Autonomic Nervous System

Imagine that your Autonomic Nervous System (ANS) has two opposing cheer squads. They wake up distinct parts of your body to respond when triggered by external events. Cheer squad 'S' is the Sympathetic Nervous System. It commands your flight, fright, freeze or fawn response. It is activated in your body when you experience trauma. When this system starts firing, your heart rate and your breathing speed up. Stress hormones start pumping through your bloodstream preparing your body to face a threat. Your body perceives you are in imminent danger, so your cheer squad is yelling - "Wake up! Danger! Wake up!"

The symptoms are: -

10. Rapid heartbeat and breathing
11. Pale or flushed skin
12. Dilated pupils
13. Trembling
14. Sweating
15. Dry Mouth
16. Nausea

Why is this happening to you?

If you are under an immediate threat, like you are being chased, this response would be useful. It gives you a burst of energy that you need to get yourself into a position of safety. That's why they call it 'nervous energy'. But if you are not in danger, it can be very damaging when your body in in this state for too long, or too often. If your 'S' cheer squad stays consistently active, it disturbs all the hormonal systems in the body. Unfortunately, this cheer squad tends to hang around long after the main event when you have suffered a loss.

Cheer squad "P" is the Parasympathetic Nervous System. It commands your rest, relax and digestion responses. It is activated in your body when you feel safe. When this system starts firing, your heart rate and your breathing slow down.

There are three steps you can take to invite the 'P' cheer squad to take over.

BREATHE

Controlled breathing regulates the adrenaline and cortisol spike of a sympathetic nervous system response. It wakes up your 'P' cheer squad. It will slow your heart rate and drop your blood pressure. As your blood vessels relax your body will go into a state of calm and healing.

When you are in trauma response and your sympathetic nervous system is dominant, your body is going to resist you. You are not going to want to do a breathing exercise. Every fibre of you will be telling you to be alert, super vigilant- looking for a tiger in the undergrowth about to pounce on you. You are safe. You are going to have to mentally override it and persist. Take control.

Remember that this is your response. You have control.

Softly affirm to yourself that you are not in danger.

"I am safe. I am safe. I am safe."

Repeat this until you feel like you can close your eyes comfortably.

Why does breathing work?

The basic science behind why breathing works, is that when your exhale is just one count longer than your inhale, the vagus nerve, that runs from your neck down through the diaphragm, sends a signal to your brain to turn up the parasympathetic nerve system and turn down the sympathetic nervous system.

You can do controlled breathing anywhere, at any time. And given the sudden onset of a trauma response, it's better to know what to do without the aid of a class so you can attend to yourself. If you feel the symptoms coming on, seek a quiet space and spend a few minutes practising-controlled breathing. I've done this exercise in a cubicle in bathrooms when out in public if I have needed to. If you can feel your body amping up, whatever the situation, excuse yourself and do this exercise.

How to do Controlled Breathing

Sit still and tall somewhere you can be as comfortable as possible. Close your eyes and begin breathing through your nose with your mouth gently closed. In just a few short minutes the production of cortisol and adrenaline will subside. The most important thing to remember is that the exhale needs to be longer than the inhale.

Try and breathe rhythmically. To breathe rhythmically means that the in breath and the out breath occur repeatedly at the same intervals.

Inhale 1-2-3 and 4.

Then exhale, 1-2-3-4-5 and 6 and then inhale

1-2-3 and 4, then exhale 1-2-3-4-5 and 6.

By following this pattern, you will set up a rhythm. Keep the volume of breath consistent and smooth as it moves in and out.

Now set a timer and breathe this way for five minutes. It will send a message to your 'S' cheer squad to pack up their pom poms and go home.

For those of you that don't feel confident doing the breathing exercise on your own, there is a wide selection available free online.

Try and follow up the breathing exercise with some physical exercise. Just some gentle movement like a walk will help your body burn the back log of trauma chemicals out of your system.

If you are feeling up to doing a breath focused activity such as yoga or a meditation class, this will help. But sometimes the planning of transport, seeing new people and other necessary obligations are roadblocks to attending classes. In the early days, it may be asking too much to expect this of yourself and that is fine. It could be a goal you could work towards within 3 to 6 months, or even a year.

NOURISH YOUR BODY

A loss can affect your appetite in many ways. You may have no appetite, or you want to eat a lot of comforting but less healthy choices. Your relationship with food may change daily and you may swing between the two approaches. Despite the emotional and psychological pain you are in, (for some the physical pain also), your body needs nourishment to keep you balanced. We function best in balance, with an even intake of what our body needs.

Why is this important right now? I can hear you now -

"With all of this going on you want me to watch what I eat?"

I do. Not in a Weight Watchers, see you in a bikini, washboard abdominal muscles on Instagram way. This is about nutrition and stability.

If you are not eating enough, you are going to suffer a lot of mood swings. And if you are only eating junk for extended periods of time, you are not going to be giving your body the fuel that it needs.

You may have gotten away with unhealthy eating patterns up until now. But the goal posts have shifted. Nothing is the same in the face of adversity. And it is crucial that you nourish yourself and eat well as you undertake processing this loss and what it means for you. You will need an even physical energy to face the challenges ahead. With a solid energy you will be physically grounded as you start to express your feelings, manage your trauma, and figure out a way to keep going.

MAKE PLANS

It helps to plan when it comes to the food you eat. Otherwise, you can lurch from sugar crash to coma in many cycles a day from quick fixes without the slow burning nutrition to keep your energy stable.

You need to think about what your choices are. Are you responsible for preparing your own food? Are you genuinely able to do it? Or are you too distressed? I still have a vivid memory of my sister-in-law Kylie putting a plate of tiny bite sized sandwiches in front of me when I was in shock after Matt's death. Looking back, I had eaten nothing for at least 48 hours.

Start small. You don't have to go gangbusters super healthy. Don't have unreasonable expectations of yourself. Just try including one piece of fruit and one or two servings of vegetables in your day.

If anyone offers to help, ask them to prep some meals and put them in containers you can put in the fridge or freezer. Tell them what you like to eat otherwise you will just end up throwing it out later. Alternatively, people can contribute to a food delivery account so you can order food that you like to eat. People who don't cook or are time poor will appreciate that they can help in this way, so don't be shy about it. It's perfectly normal to accept support while you are vulnerable.

If you don't have anyone offering that level of support, you have 5 minutes to feel sad about it, then let it go. Hit up the prepared meals section of the supermarket. There are plenty of choices with a good variety of foods that are quite nutritious that you can choose from. What you don't want is to not be hungry for dinner, then open a party size pack of corn chips late at night and graze on junk food.

If you are struggling to eat at all I get it. Often the cortisol can disrupt your appetite and any solids feel like they are gagging you and your stomach is queasy. Get yourself some bulk packs of protein shakes in a neutral flavour like vanilla. They will satiate your hunger pangs and stop you from feeling lightheaded and nauseous. Quick tip. Bananas are your friend. Quick, easy, ready to go with lots of good nutrients.

If you find yourself in the above-mentioned corn chip scenario, make yourself some two-minute noodles. The flavour sachets aren't great to eat all the time, but you can season plain ones with a little soy and sesame oil. They aren't an 'everyday' food - but serve a purpose if you are feeling sick because you have a gnawing belly hunger.

Coffee. For a lot of people, the idea of starting the day without coffee is an impossibility. That's understandable. But remember that caffeine can amplify any anxiety you are feeling. It is also an appetite suppressant. Too much coffee can leave you jittery and nauseous. Be mindful of the effect your coffee intake is having on you. If you find that after drinking it you start experiencing racing thoughts, sweaty palms, and emotional swings, assess whether it's helpful to consume at the moment. You can return to it later, just decide to not add this drug to the mix while you are in the loss state.

Alcohol. Alcohol will suppress your appetite and is a known depressant. Initially alcohol has a stimulant effect on the body, but after a certain amount it acts as a depressant on the central nervous system and messes with your judgement and perception. There's kind of enough going on right now without adding regretful drunk decisions to the mix.

My experience had me trapped with drinking as everyone around me were drinkers and choosing to abstain was really threatening to others. It's very revealing to be the only sober person at a function and watch how alcohol affects people. So, I never openly said I wasn't drinking. I would accept the drink alongside a huge glass of mineral water and just let it sit.

Sometimes alcohol loosens people up to share their feelings and drinking acts as a cathartic release. This is not a healthy way to 'share and purge'. Often the remembering becomes lost again as you wake up with a pounding head and too many gaps in the timeline. In the next three chapters you will gain the skills to artfully access your feelings without substances and navigate others' feelings and their reactions to your feelings. The rule I have for drinking to keep myself safe is: -

"Only drink to celebrate. Only drink when you are feeling happy."

Over ten years on, this is still applicable.

Avoid dehydration. Aim for at least 8-10 glasses of water a day. Start every morning with a glass before breakfast. One way to keep the fluids up is to buy a water bottle and get used to keeping it with you. Drinking water will become second nature and you will be surprised at how much better you feel when you are fully hydrated. People don't bang on about it for nothing.

Water is good for you. Especially if you are crying a lot. With trauma spikes you also sweat a lot so it's important to keep replacing your fluids. If you are thirsty - you are already dehydrated. You don't want to get too thirsty before you amend the situation.

Did you know that a headache is a symptom of dehydration? If you have a headache, drink a couple of glasses of water and wait 15 minutes before you go reaching for any tablets. You may not need them.

SLEEP

Trauma and grief cause sleep problems, and sleep problems make your symptoms worse. You feel it in your muscles, and it is hard to keep going every day. It's a tough cycle where you feel overwhelmed and exhausted and yet you can't sleep. This cycle leaves you tired all the time, and it is difficult to function.

A lack of good sleep can cause other problems too like depression and weight gain. Exhaustion increases your risk of car accidents and can also weaken your immune system.

Insomnia is a natural symptom of trauma and grief. Lying in the dark, your thoughts and emotions take over and it is difficult to soothe yourself to sleep. And when you finally fall asleep, it is usually a 'dead sleep' that you wake up from even more exhausted.

By treating your sleep difficulties, you are going to feel better, and you are going to start to feel more alive again because you are well rested. You will have enough energy to deal with whatever it is that you must deal with that day.

You are going to train yourself to fall asleep. The last time you did it was when you were a baby, and you don't remember. You are experiencing the same feeling of being abandoned. When your mother left the room, you had to self-soothe because she wasn't there anymore. And now you are suffering from the same problem. Being truly alone in your grief is as instinctive and harsh as it can get. Let's look at some practical steps you can take.

Firstly, you need to set the scene. In the same way you would if you were putting an infant to sleep.

Consider a new mattress if you need one and if you can afford it. If not, a memory foam topper is a less expensive way to make your bed more comfortable.

Rearrange the room. If you are grieving because you have lost the person you shared the room with, remove anything in the space that triggers you emotionally. Photos and personal belongings can be boxed up and put out of sight in a cupboard or the garage. You don't have to throw anything out. Just make your restful space calm and relaxing. You do not want to be sleeping in a museum.

Make sure that the room is cool, dark, and quiet. Remove electronics from the room. No screens. No TV, no tablets, no computers, no smart phone. Get yourself an old school alarm clock and charge your phone in the living room.

Invest in some new bed linen. Bamboo sheets are soft and comfortable. (And environmentally responsible).

Change the lighting. Use a lamp with a low wattage. Soften it all so it is a refuge where you want to go to retreat and rest.

Stick to consistent times of when you go to bed and when you wake up every day. Don't beat yourself up if you can't always do this, but you will start feel better if you create a healthy sleep 'rhythm' in your day-to-day life.

As mentioned before, watch the caffeine and alcohol intake. Black and green tea both have caffeine also.

Try to limit daytime naps. It can be tempting to disappear into unconsciousness when you are overwhelmed and burnt out. Stay awake. Distract yourself with a book or a film or cooking. Nothing too strenuous. Just a gentle distraction when your energy is low to stop you from sleeping. Try and get 10-15 minutes of direct sun a day to regulate your circadian rhythm. All creatures have a circadian rhythm that is affected by light and darkness. Even amoebae. Sunlight stimulates melatonin that helps you sleep. Do the rhythmic breathing exercises before going to bed.

If you have a bathtub, get hold of some magnesium salts and have a 20-minute soak every night before bed. It will relax and soothe you, putting you in the right mood to drift off. If you don't have a bathtub, take a magnesium supplement. Magnesium is known to reduce muscle tension, improve sleep and address anxiety and depression.

If you find that you are still restless and are tossing and turning and you don't fall away, get up. Make yourself some herbal tea and read a book. Why books? Reading books tires and focuses the brain in a way that scrolling soundbites doesn't. Reading requires you to use multiple areas of the brain in a coordinated way. No screens. You have already put those away for the night. Stick with the intention of reducing distraction so you are calm enough to sleep. Learn to soothe yourself in a way that's reflective and not about distraction.

If you try all these suggestions and are still struggling to get to sleep, you should check in with your primary health care provider and get some bloodwork done. You may be low on certain vitamins and minerals that affect your ability to sleep.

Usually, the first line of treatment for insomnia from most doctors will be to give you pills or suggest pills. Sleeping pills are powerful hypnotics that are recommended for a very brief window of time that's usually less than a month. They are often over prescribed. You will get a chemical knockout and they will get you to sleep. But once those pills runout, what are you going to do? This is a crazy rabbit hole that many people end up down. You may become addicted. And if not addicted, psychologically dependent on a quick way to get to sleep.

Another issue with these meds is how they mess with the processing your subconscious mind is doing to help you heal and move forward in time from your loss. If you have black hole drug sleep every night, none of this important work happens. When you sleep naturally, your subconscious is taking inventory on the day's experiences, observations, and emotional responses. Like moving all these random files and open windows sitting on your screen and putting them in their rightful places where they belong. With the drugged sleep - that screen stays a mess, with thoughts and ideas all half hanging out of the recesses of your mind.

Educate yourself about the risks and side effects of any psychoactive medication that you are prescribed. I do not recommend using them unless they are strictly monitored and for a brief necessary intervention.

Find out what they are for. What mechanism they work on in your brain. How long you should be on them. The pros AND the cons. Medications will affect your temperament, your appetite, your ability to drive, your libido. In short, everything about you. Got that? Not just sleep.

RETREAT

If you find yourself around people and start experiencing that feeling of being abandoned or misunderstood, choose to retreat. Some people will prove to be supportive allies, others you may never speak to or hear from again. And some will not know how to behave and keep triggering you with insensitive questions or comments. We are going to address this in greater detail from Chapter 5 onwards.

Why retreat?

It is a fundamental survival mechanism to avoid discomfort. To avoid pain and distress. Every interaction you have is an exchange of energy. Your status as a person who is suffering now affects the systems within which you are living.

Imagine a mobile with all the parts carefully balanced and slowly orbiting around each other. Now imagine if one of those pieces is swapped out for a heavier one. The mobile lurches wildly, the pieces crashing into each other. The same is happening in your family circle and your social circle. Everyone is scrambling to find out where they are in the mobile now it is out of balance.

Sometimes it feels like people are purposefully avoiding you. It's not personal. They most likely have poor coping skills or little to offer.

Often the people who feel obligated to stand by you are angry at you at an unconscious level that they aren't even aware of. They just feel so terribly bad about your situation. And frustrated that they can't 'fix' it. Nothing that they do can solve this and they feel helpless. The balance of the system has been upset and everyone is scrambling to find equilibrium in this new reality.

Pay close attention to how you feel around others. Monitor this. Don't go into the brain heavy details of the hows and the whys. Of what people said or did. You are not going to solve other people and you are not going to find meaning in what's going on for them. Stay focused on you. Stay in the feeling, in your gut. Not in the thinking. Focus on your feeling state. Because the way people are behaving around you, the way that they are responding to you, is ABSOLUTELY NOT ABOUT YOU. It is about them. It is their inability to cope with what is going on.

Our brains are problem-solving machines. Our brains are also meaning making machines. But they don't have the full picture yet. They are working on the fly and confused by the pattern break. In this time, after your life has been upended, there has been a pattern break. It freaks the people around you out.

Does spending time around a particular person leave you feeling better or worse afterwards? Is the interaction heavy? Or light? Do you feel like you are defending your state or being supported? If the energy is not good for you, retreat. You can revisit at a later point in time if you feel obligated.

Be full of care for yourself right now. Be careful. Start becoming conscious of how you are treating your body. Good decisions and choices will support you while you are suffering.

Focus on your felt state and monitor what is happening physically.

CHECKLIST OF STEPS TO TAKE

a) If you can feel trauma spike symptoms coming on, attend to it and do the breathing exercises.

b) The right nutrition will nourish you. There is more comfort in even energy than comfort food.

c) Use the strategies listed to ensure sleep and that you are rested without using medication.

d) Retreat from social interactions you find yourself in if they are triggering you.

There is a care worksheet at the end of each chapter that will remind you to keep checking in with how well you are doing.

By filling it in you will start to see patterns and that will help you to see where you need to pay more attention or seek more support. If you don't want to write in the book, consider buying an exercise book to use while you are taking yourself through this process.

The above steps are the base upon which all this work will take place. You cannot escape your embodied reality and must be vigilant in supporting your physical needs.

WEEK DATE:	MONDAY	TUESDAY	WEDNESDAY	THURSDAY	FRIDAY	SATURDAY	SUNDAY
BREATHE	YES x	YES x	YES x	YES x	YES x	YES x	YES x
	NO	NO	NO	NO	NO	NO	NO
EATING	OKAY NOT ENOUGH TOO MUCH	OKAY NOT ENOUGH TOO MUCH	OKAY NOT ENOUGH TOO MUCH	OKAY NOT ENOUGH TOO MUCH	OKAY NOT ENOUGH TOO MUCH	OKAY NOT ENOUGH TOO MUCH	OKAY NOT ENOUGH TOO MUCH
FLUIDS	OKAY NOT ENOUGH	OKAY NOT ENOUGH	OKAY NOT ENOUGH	OKAY NOT ENOUGH	OKAY NOT ENOUGH	OKAY NOT ENOUGH	OKAY NOT ENOUGH
SLEEP	OKAY NOT ENOUGH TOO MUCH	OKAY NOT ENOUGH TOO MUCH	OKAY NOT ENOUGH TOO MUCH	OKAY NOT ENOUGH TOO MUCH	OKAY NOT ENOUGH TOO MUCH	OKAY NOT ENOUGH TOO MUCH	OKAY NOT ENOUGH TOO MUCH
INTERACT	WHO? FELT GOOD FELT BAD	WHO? FELT GOOD FELT BAD	WHO? FELT GOOD FELT BAD	WHO? FELT GOOD FELT BAD	WHO? FELT GOOD FELT BAD	WHO? FELT GOOD FELT BAD	WHO? FELT GOOD FELT BAD

YOU

ONE
THE CRUCIBLE - PROCESSING EMOTIONS

Emotions are extremely sophisticated biological survival tools that we share with all mammals. They are an inbuilt GPS system designed to keep us safe. We can only utilise them to our best advantage if we are able to understand the messages that they are sending us. Then we can respond to the cue appropriately. There are eight primary emotions that we share with other mammals. They are: -

> Sadness
> Anger
> Disgust
> Fear
> Anticipation
> Surprise
> Trust
> Joy

Sadness, Anger, Disgust, Fear and Surprise are all experienced as negative sensations in our body. They trigger specific physical responses that make us feel uncomfortable. They usually turn up together in a group or subgroup. Often the emotions themselves are considered by the one experiencing them as a problem rather than as a message to protect them.

If you go to the doctor and describe yourself as anxious and depressed, they will give you pills to flatten your affect. The medicine will help you in managing the unpleasant symptoms you are experiencing with negative emotions.

What medicine won't explore is you. Your emotional literacy. Your emotional terrain. The why behind the feelings that you are having. These emotions, these survival tools will help you move towards the positive in your life. Because when you process the felt sensations you can let go of them and move forward. You will feel lighter, with a better understanding of how your emotions work. You will learn to trust and appreciate them rather than feel trapped in them or overwhelmed by them.

Anticipation, Trust, and Joy are all positive felt sensations in the body. When you look at the balance of emotions you can see that it is not reasonable to expect people to feel good all the time. Nature doesn't really care if you are happy or not. It just wants you to survive, and therefore our survival tools (emotions) are there to keep us safe.

When we are living beyond our survival and can bask in Trust, Joy, and Anticipation, we experience positive physical sensations. Our bodies are flooded with endorphins and dopamine. These are our inbuilt pleasure centre.

So how do we experience more of these moments? They can't be experienced alongside the negative emotions. It is physiologically impossible. To feel good, every time one of these negatively felt emotions surfaces it needs to be cross-examined.

Why are you feeling it? What is it in relation to? Is it an old feeling you keep revisiting? Is it a valid and reasonable response? How is it keeping you safe? Is it habitual? Is it your expectation that is the problem? These are all big questions.

Emotional literacy is an easy skill to gain. To become fluent, you must stay curious and keep asking questions about your survival response. It will take time and patience. You must be willing to address a lifetime of suppression and grieving for not listening to your own heart. For ignoring your gut instincts. If I can offer any consolation, you were conditioned to work more from logic and less from your emotions. It can be undone. You will become very skilled at reflection and realignment. While you are alive, no matter how dark life feels, there is always possibility and there is always hope. But you must be willing to face the emotions. You must start checking in with the physical, psychological, and emotional responses you have to the people and events in your life.

And be prepared to change. Because if nothing changes? Nothing changes.

Your emotions are expressed in response to events that affect you directly, and also in response to how others respond to your emotional needs. We are pack animals. And to be isolated or excluded from the pack can have extreme mental health consequences. When you are blindsided, it can set off a chain reaction in the people around you. They can't disappear your pain. You may find you are surrounded by people that are not really your allies. For the sake of politeness, you are investing in people that may trigger you daily, even hourly, in ways that affect your ability to process your emotions.

We'll look at those distinct kinds of empathy with more depth in Chapter 7.

Sadness

Sadness looks and feels like you are suffering mental, physical, or emotional pain. Sadness the 'survival tool' is felt when we experience loss. We process it in our minds as separation from that which we enjoy. It feels like abandonment. Recognising the abandonment, we feel sadness and we cry. We can resolve sadness by reattaching to what it is that we have lost. But this isn't always possible. Sadness has purpose. It tells us what is of value to us in our lives.

Sadness connects us to those we love, including ourselves.

> I am feeling sad because I have lost…
> And what I have lost was important to me.

Reflect on your sadness. Is it a response to a singular and isolated event? We have a habit of ignoring or suppressing our responses until we reach a critical tipping point. Sometimes we can have a sadness response that seems excessive to the event.

This is because it is driven by other feelings of sadness that have built over time and have remained trapped inside you unexpressed.

It is as if you no longer have space to hold the pain anymore and it needs release. Often people ignore their feelings of sadness. They use films or music or other people's tragedies to express this important survival signal because they don't know how to be sad for themselves.

Our modern culture is obsessed with happiness. The promise of a golden mirage that you might someday reach and live 'happily ever after'. The fairy tale delusion.

But our lives are always in flux. Within us. Outside of us. In our immediate circumstance and our global circumstance. We are all connected. This is why our emotions are so fluid and can change quickly. It is possible to move through all our primary emotions in a day. Even a morning!

There is a physiological release that we experience when we cry. We feel relief. Relief at shifting to a bigger truth of what matters to us. When we grieve it sharpens our focus. Our lives become more vivid. Real. Bruce Lee once said,

> "Sorrows are our best educator. A man can see further through a tear than a telescope."

Close your eyes and recall what is making you sad. Where do you feel sadness in your body? Is it an ache in your chest? A heaviness in your eyes? A tightening in your throat? Does your mouth tighten and grimace? Maybe your scalp prickles. There are many physical cues unique to our experience of sadness.

Sadness can look like and feel like unhappiness, sorrow, disappointment, shame, neglect, dejection, regret, depression, misery, cheerlessness, downheartedness, despondency, despair, desolation, wretchedness, glumness, gloom, dolefulness, melancholy, low spirits, mournfulness, woe, broken-heartedness, heartache, grief, down, disconsolation, dismalness, disadvantage, helplessness and sympathy.

This is by no means an exhaustive list of words to describe how sadness looks and feels. Can you think of any other words that describe your feelings of sadness?

Anger

Anger looks and feels like you are suffering irritation. Anger the 'survival tool' is felt when we are confronted with an obstacle. We process it as conflict. Recognising conflict, we feel anger and attack. We resolve anger by destroying the obstacle. But as we know, this isn't always possible. Anger has purpose. It tells us what is stopping us from getting what we want. Anger fuels us to fight against problems.

I am feeling anger because…
And this is preventing me from getting what I want.

Reflect on your anger. Is it a response to a singular and isolated event? We have a habit of ignoring or suppressing our anger responses until we end up lashing out. Sometimes we can have an anger response that seems excessive to the event. This is because it is driven by feelings of anger that have built up over time and have remained trapped inside you. It's as if you no longer have space to hold the anger anymore and it needs release. Often people ignore their feelings of anger, and they use films or music or other people's injustices to express this important survival signal because they don't know how to own their anger. Our modern culture is obsessed with righteous anger as if it is an emotion expressed without consequences.

There is always a consequence to anger. Withholding its expression and internalising it can create all sorts of health issues like hypertension and heightened cortisol levels. Over time those elevated stress chemicals can affect your physical health. But expressing it in ways that other people find threatening can also leave you isolated and disconnected.

Expressing anger in uncontrolled ways can escalate situations and they can become very violent quickly. It is important to respond to your anger. It is important to do this in isolation before considering a response. A spontaneous reaction could create an unintended consequence.

Be wary of people who hum with anger. They are not interested in resolving their anger. They are using it as fuel to move through the world. The tension of their contained conflict is exhausting.

All conflict must eventually be resolved. Or walked away from. The action of retreat is a valid form of resolving anger. At the very least in the safety of retreat the feeling of anger can be explored with curiosity. Reflecting on it can help you to put solid boundaries in place to protect yourself from conflict.

Anger is also a highly infectious emotion. Often you can be holding onto another's anger and hurting yourself. Is it your anger? Perhaps it is an emotional response that you learned from your parents. Is it helpful? Is it creating determination and energy? Or do you feel trapped and exhausted by it? What does it feel like in your body? Is it like a fever? Does your face become hot and prickly? Do you feel violent? Do you want to cry? We all have our own unique physical cues that tell us when we are angry.

Anger can look and feel like exasperation, rage, envy, torment, acrimony, hatred, impatience, indignation, animosity, ire, outrage, passion, antagonism, resentment, annoyance, abuse, violence, chagrin, displeasure, belligerence, enmity, fury, explosiveness. This is by no means an exhaustive list of words to describe what anger looks and feels like. Can you think of any other words that describe your feelings of anger?

Disgust

Disgust looks and feels like you are experiencing revulsion.

Disgust the 'survival tool' is felt when we experience something that is highly toxic and dangerous. Recognising poison, we feel disgusted, and we reject it. We resolve disgust by rejecting what is toxic to us. Sometimes this is difficult. Disgust has purpose. It tells us what is toxic and dangerous to us. Disgust tells us to reject what is unhealthy. Often it can be a precursor to the sadness of loss.

When we are affected by disgusting behaviour that is toxic, we must relinquish the person who treats us in this way. We feel sadness after the disgust when we come to realise that this person is no good for us. That they do not have our best interests at heart.

Disgust can also be felt before anger. Sometimes there is a relationship between these survival emotions that might be a pattern.

I am feeling disgusted because... and it is unhealthy for me.

Disgust can look and feel like contempt, repulsion, distaste, aversion, loathing, and boredom. This is by no means an exhaustive list of what disgust looks or feels like. Can you think of any other words that might describe your feelings of disgust?

Fear

Fear looks and feels like you are experiencing terror or nervousness and everything in between. It may be either the suddenness of horror, or the slow burn of nervousness but with the same root. Fear the 'survival tool' is felt when we experience a threat. We process it as danger. Recognising danger, our felt sensation is fear, and we escape. We resolve fear by escaping to safety. This isn't always possible. Fear has purpose. It tells us when we need to seek protection and withdraw or retreat.

Fear protects us from danger. When we suppress fear and leave our potential threats unexamined or unresolved, the fear nests inside of us. It becomes low level anxiety at its least damaging, and hyper vigilance and dissociation at its most destructive.

I am fearful because... and this situation is dangerous for me.

Fear can look and feel like horror, alarm, shock, fright, terror, panic, hysteria, and mortification. Fear can also look and feel like anxiety, tenseness, uneasiness, apprehension, worry, distress, and dread. Can you think of any other words that might describe your feelings of fear?

Anticipation

Anticipation looks and feels like interest that may cause pleasure or anxiety. Anticipation the 'survival tool' is felt when we are in unfamiliar territory. We approach it with curiosity to get our bearings. Recognising our curiosity, we feel anticipation and start to map the fresh territory. We resolve anticipation by gaining knowledge of the fresh territory. What is foreign becomes familiar. This happens with people, places, and events. Anticipation has purpose. It tells us what we need to know in a new situation. Anticipation prepares us to look forward and plan.

Hyper vigilance is a form of anxiety. If it escalates to anxiety, it becomes difficult to process the latest information clearly. Anxiety often prevents people from new experiences as the anticipation is difficult to manage and filled with dread. This is where the need to control everything can become destructive.

I am anticipating... and I need to plan for this. I can do this within reason but should also allow room for uncertainty.

Anticipation can look and feel like expectancy, curiosity, vigilance, and excitement. Can you think of any other words that might describe your feelings of anticipation?

Surprise

Surprise looks and feels like a shock. At its mildest it is a distraction. Surprise the 'survival tool' is felt when we experience an unexpected event. We process it firstly by asking,

"What's that?"

Recognising the shock of the unexpected, we feel surprised, and we resolve that surprise by freezing. Freezing gives us time to compute. By freezing we create an opportunity to reorient.

Surprise has purpose. Surprise shows us what our preconceived expectations are. How we function in response to patterns and consistency.

Surprise also reminds us that we cannot know the future. Surprise helps us to focus on new situations.

I feel surprised by... and it was unexpected.

Shock is a term for trauma that doesn't get used so much these days. What is now described as PTSD (post-traumatic stress disorder) used to be called shell shock when describing the trauma that war veterans returned home with. When people would be in accidents or experience a terrible tragedy, they would go into 'shock'. Shock affects our limbic system. It triggers our amygdala and affects our ability to think clearly.

Surprise can look and feel like amazement, astonishment or shock. Can you think of any other words that might describe your feelings of surprise?

Trust

Trust looks and feels like acceptance. Trust the 'survival tool' is felt when we experience connection. We process this connection as alliance. Recognising alliance, we feel trust and groom and deepen the connection. We experience trust as support.

Trust has purpose. It tells us who is supportive in our lives. Trust connects us to people who can help.

I trust...   because they can help me and choose to help me.

Trust looks and feels like admiration, affection, lust, longing, and love. Can you think of any other words that might describe your feelings of trust?

Joy

Joy looks and feels like cheerfulness. Joy the 'survival tool' is felt when we experience expansion. We process this as want. We want more of this experience because it feels good. Recognising this desire, we feel joy and keep and repeat the experience. We experience joy as gaining personal resources. These resources are primarily related to connection. To others, and to personal dreams and desires. Joy has purpose. It tells us who and what enhances our lived experience. Joy tells us what is important to us.

I am joyful when... and this matters to me.

Joy also looks and feels like zest, contentment, pride, optimism, enthralment, and relief. Can you think of any other words that might describe your feelings of joy?

IMPORTANT

Make sure that you have time on the other side of these exercises to relax and rest. You may feel quite tired or emotionally drained. Start your self-care by giving yourself this time to process.

Do you have food ready for the next meal? A quiet space to rest? Someone who can mind people or animals you may be responsible for? This is deep work designed to shift and release stuck feelings, so it will take far more energy than you might think.

Exercise 1 - Emotional Profile

Read each of the following lists that describes one of the 8 primary emotions and highlight or tick the ones you are experiencing right now. Don't overthink it. Just own it. Don't be self-conscious. This exercise is for you, and you alone. If you don't want anyone to see what you are recording, you can write them out separately on a piece of paper and discard it later.

We spend so much time in our minds. It is our secret space where we hide our thoughts. I want you to acknowledge these feelings mentally AND physically by recording them. Remember, they are providing you with especially valuable information. Data about your emotional terrain if you like.

Each of these descriptions has been divided into subgroups. The goal here is for you to break apart these monumental overreaching emotions of sad, or angry, and see the nuance in the language. Each manifestation of the primary emotions will pertain to different situations, circumstances, and people. And you are feeling them all at once.

Go for it. You may only mark off a couple. You may mark all of them off and add some more of your own.

If you are someone who doesn't pay attention to their emotional state until the wheels start falling off everything, this may feel intense. Again, these are by no means exhaustive lists.

These are exercises that accelerate your emotional literacy every day. The more you do them, the better you get. As you work through the different steps each week, keep coming back to this initial step.

Remember, your feelings are your biological survival toolkit. They will inform the actions you need to take to stay safe while you are vulnerable.

SUFFERING
hurt
anguish
suffering
agony

SADNESS
grief
unhappiness
glumness
gloom
hopelessness
despair
depression
sorrow
woe
misery
melancholy

NEGLECT
alienation
isolation
neglect
loneliness
rejection
homesickness
defeat
dejection
insecurity
embarrassment
humiliation & insult

SHAME
regret
remorse
guilt
shame

DISAPPOINTMENT
displeasure
dismay
disappointment

SYMPATHY
pity
sympathy

THE PURPOSE OF OUR 8 PRIMARY EMOTIONS AND HOW TO WORK WITH THEM.

SADNESS connects us to those we love. You have just expanded on all the different ways that sadness is being felt for you. There are stories and incidents connected to each of the words that you marked off the list.

We are now going to connect each of these descriptions of sadness with the reason why you are feeling it. It may be shame. It may be isolation.

I feel sad.
My sadness feels like shame because...
My sadness feels like isolation because...

Write these out in your exercise book. You can tear the pages into pieces or burn them when you are done. It is not the 'evidence' of your feelings that is important. It is the action of processing them, naming them and connecting them. Eventually this process will become internalized and easy. But for now, writing them out will best grow your emotional literacy.

IRRITATION
aggravation
irritation
agitation
annoyance
grouchiness
grumpiness

EXASPERATION
exasperation
frustration

TORMENT
torment

ENVY
jealousy
envy

RAGE
anger
rage
outrage
fury
wrath
hostility
ferocity
bitterness
hate
loathing
scorn
spite
vengefulness
dislike
resentment

DISGUST
contempt
disgust
revulsion

We are going to repeat the process again with each primary emotion.

ANGER fuels us to fight against problems. You have just expanded on all the different ways that anger is being felt for you. There are stories and incidents connected to each of the words that you marked off the list.

We are now going to connect each of these descriptions of anger with the reason why you are feeling it. It may be exasperation. It maybe annoyance.

>I feel angry because...
>I feel exasperated because...
>I feel annoyed because...

DISGUST tells us to reject what is unhealthy.

>I feel disgusted because...
>I feel contempt because...

NERVOUSNESS
anxiety
nervousness
tenseness
uneasiness
apprehension
worry
distress
dread

HORROR
alarm
shock
fear
fright
horror
terror
panic
hysteria
mortification

amazement surprise astonishment

FEAR protects us from danger. What is the 'because' of your fear?

> I feel fearful because...
> I feel anxious because...
> I am uneasy because...

Keep going. Keep unpacking the 'why' behind the feeling. There is purpose to your feelings. They are powerful and protective.

SURPRISE helps us focus on new situations.

> I feel surprised because...
> I am shocked because...

No one needs to read this but you. You don't need to share this information with anyone else. Here, you are testing your compass. Owning the feelings and attributing them to your unique situation. Listening to them and responding accordingly will keep you safe.

AFFECTION	LUST	LONGING
adoration	desire	longing
affection	lust	
love	passion	
fondness	infatuation	
liking	arousal	
attraction		
caring		
tenderness		
compassion		
sentimentality		

interest   curiosity   vigilance

TRUST connects us to people who can help.

> I feel trust because...
> I feel affection because...

These positive emotions may be difficult to access while you are feeling the 'safety emotions' negatively in your body.

I want you to access your memories as a benchmark for you to complete this exercise. Be aware that exploring memories of these emotions about someone you have lost may bring up its own sadness that you can no longer experience them in the present. Hold tight to the memory of these sensations though. Later they will resurface in unexpected ways.

ANTICIPATION prepares us to look forward and plan.

> I feel anticipation because...
> I feel curious because...
> I feel vigilant because...

CHEERFULNESS

amusement, gladness, bliss, cheerfulness, gaiety, glee, jolliness, joviality, joy, delight, enjoyment, gladness, happiness, jubilation, elation, satisfaction, ecstasy, euphoria

CONTENTMENT

contentment
pleasure

RELIEF

relief

ZEST

enthusiasm
zeal
zest
excitement
thrill
exhilaration

PRIDE

triumph
pride

OPTIMISM

eagerness
hope
optimism

ENTHRALMENT

enthralment
rapture

JOY reminds us of what is important. What is important to you?

> I feel joyful because...
> I feel relief because...
> I feel contentment because...

Again, these can be reflections and memories and not just current feelings. It might be difficult to access your joy while you are experiencing loss. What is important is that you tease out all the different ways you have, can and will experience joy.

Remember to fill out your self-care diary this week to check your patterns of care and what kind of support you may need.

WEEK DATE:	MONDAY	TUESDAY	WEDNESDAY	THURSDAY	FRIDAY	SATURDAY	SUNDAY
BREATHE	YES x NO	YES x NO	YES x NO	YES x NO	YES x NO	YES x NO	YES x NO
EATING	OKAY NOT ENOUGH TOO MUCH	OKAY NOT ENOUGH TOO MUCH	OKAY NOT ENOUGH TOO MUCH	OKAY NOT ENOUGH TOO MUCH	OKAY NOT ENOUGH TOO MUCH	OKAY NOT ENOUGH TOO MUCH	OKAY NOT ENOUGH TOO MUCH
FLUIDS	OKAY NOT ENOUGH	OKAY NOT ENOUGH	OKAY NOT ENOUGH	OKAY NOT ENOUGH	OKAY NOT ENOUGH	OKAY NOT ENOUGH	OKAY NOT ENOUGH
SLEEP	OKAY NOT ENOUGH TOO MUCH	OKAY NOT ENOUGH TOO MUCH	OKAY NOT ENOUGH TOO MUCH	OKAY NOT ENOUGH TOO MUCH	OKAY NOT ENOUGH TOO MUCH	OKAY NOT ENOUGH TOO MUCH	OKAY NOT ENOUGH TOO MUCH
INTERACT	WHO? FELT GOOD FELT BAD	WHO? FELT GOOD FELT BAD	WHO? FELT GOOD FELT BAD	WHO? FELT GOOD FELT BAD	WHO? FELT GOOD FELT BAD	WHO? FELT GOOD FELT BAD	WHO? FELT GOOD FELT BAD

Process

8 primary emotions are survival responses of organisms at all evolutionary levels

EVENT	THOUGHT	EMOTION	BEHAVIOUR	FUNCTION
THREAT	DANGER	FEAR	ESCAPE	SAFETY
LOSS	ABANDONMENT	SADNESS	CRY	REATTACH TO LOST
UNEXPECTED	WHAT IS IT?	SURPRISE	STOP	TIME TO ORIENT
UNPALATABLE	POISON	DISGUST	VOMIT	EJECT POISON
OBSTACLE	ENEMY	ANGER	ATTACK	DESTROY OBSTACLE
NEW TERRITORY	EXAMINE	ANTICIPATION	MAP	KNOWLEDGE OF TERRITORY
CONNECTION	FRIEND	TRUST	GROOM	MUTUAL SUPPORT
GAIN	POSSESS	JOY	RETAIN	GAIN

Two
The Birdseye - Stretching The Story

Everyone uses stories to make sense of their lives. Telling stories is about linking the past, the present, and the future in a way that makes sense to you. Your story that you tell is dependent on many things, but it is uniquely yours.

Your stories are not about nailing down 'the truth'. They are about clarifying your perspective in each situation. You need a perspective at a specific point in time. And even this perspective is always changing. You shift between your memories and your feelings. The events that you are currently experiencing in your life also helps shape your perspective.

Right now, in the pain that you're in, everything feels extremely complicated. But how you got here? What happened to you?

It's remarkably simple. The cause and effect can be described in a few words. You are suffering the pain of loss. Now we cannot go back in time and change what's happened to you. We cannot time travel. What is done cannot be undone.

When you become stuck in dark feelings, when you're caught in a problem-saturated story, it feels dense, heavy, fractured, and difficult. It can be hard to see beyond the despair.

Grief is a state that demands constant evaluation and revision of what matters to you. To let what is lost slowly go and quietly take up residence in the past. To explore the way back from immediate trauma to living in unknown potential futures. And in doing so reclaim those parts of yourself that you have been neglecting or you did not know existed.

The value of your story lays in finding out where you are so you can move forward. Sometimes reality is too complex, and stories can help to give it form. By reflecting on your perspective of a situation it can help you through this dark time where there really are no words to describe what you are going through.

Imagine your mind as a cross section of sandstone, with all the different layers of sediment, one on top of the other. Each is its own story. But how reliable are our stories? How do our memories work? For example, when we look at old photos of our childhood. Do we remember the actual event? Or is the memory embedded in the photo that recorded it? The ways our brains and our memories work are very murky.

What I'm going to ask you to do is to get back to basics. When you are recalling moments and there are feelings that are coming up alongside it, I want you to feel into the divergence. When you're in a story and you can feel it thickening and becoming crowded, take a pause. Stop. Because right there, is a turn of phrase that is your friend, and it will simplify everything. That phrase is,

"But that's another story."

This simple observation will pace the processing for you. Slow it down. It will help you come to terms with the stories around you, and the stories inside of you and the ability to see the difference between them.

Because we can think harder and harder about the problem our brain is desperate to solve and still not produce any simple solutions that will make our hearts lighter. We can outthink our unhelpful thoughts with time, effort and understanding, but we can't outthink our feelings.

Where there is a complex story, there is a dense layer of feelings. And where there is a dense layer of feelings there is always a complex story.

Sensory Triggers

Sometimes the story turns up with a sensory experience. It might be a smell, or a sound. Maybe a car you drive by or a t-shirt someone used to wear or seeing their favourite colour. Perhaps you hear a song that was part of your story together. Or a texture that links to a moment in time and it has its own story attached. That one sensory experience is a part of your dense story.

These are the stories without words. They become a swirling sensation of hindsight, recollection, memories, wishes, and intuition. They can become lost in translation.

The Value of Stories

There is so much possibility in the story we tell ourselves.

There are so many options in the story that we can live. Telling yourself the most supportive story can change your life. Your future. Right now, it's as if you are in the centre of a giant spider web of stories. There are all these different destination points from where you are. Imagine that each connected story is a dewdrop on that spider web. Each of these dewdrops holds countless stories inside of it. And inside every dew drop you can look at the story differently and form a distinct perspective.

Remember that this new life, whether you want it or not, is going to cost you your old one because it is a different story.

I don't know how many of you watch TED talks. They are marketed as the 'Talks that will change your life'. There are interesting people that give TED talks. People who tell their stories and talk about a life-changing event that happened to them. There is always an 'aha! moment' that they reached that significantly changed them. We can see how this moment was life changing for that person. It informs a sense of well-being in us to see how another responded to a challenge.

But do we honestly ever act on somebody else's 'aha! moment?' Or do we enjoy seeing somebody else experience it and let the glow fade? It is exceedingly difficult to act on an 'aha! moment' from somebody else's life. You can witness it, but you need to figure out a way that you can live your own TED talk.

To find your own 'Aha' moment.

What TED talks are showing you is that change is possible. That adversity can be overcome.

What is your insight about your situation that's going to inform your life going forward?

Let's pin down the very bare bones of where you are right now. You are the actor in the centre of your own stage. Grieving. What's the plot that got you here? Was it death or divorce or breakdown? Ageing, natural disaster or illness?

B-Roll

For those of you who haven't heard this term before, B-Roll is what fills up the screen between the action and the plot when you are making a film. It's the 'feel' of a movie.

You might believe at first that it's a story in and of itself but it's just there for context and detail around the action that drives the plot. A filler if you like. Sometimes it can be confusing to figure out what is the true plot line of a story.

You need to map it out to see what is just B-Roll in your life at the moment, and what is really going on centre stage. What is the plot?

A helpful way to differentiate is to ask whether that part of the story is going to matter to you in five years. An awful lot falls away when you use the five-year glasses. Keep homing in on what the real action is for you. What is happening centre stage for you? What is it that you are going to decide to leave on the cutting room floor?

If it does need to come up again, eventually it will. But right now, if it isn't helpful to you, let it fall. You can pick it up again later. Remember this is an opportunity for you to say,

"But that's another story."

That other story is your B-Roll.

Examples of B-Roll are: - other people's grief, other people's motivations, other people's coping mechanisms like alcohol or drugs. There is NO ENERGY in your tank to rescue anyone else right now. And anyone that expects this of you is failing you.

Paradox

Allow room for paradox in your story. Following a blindside there are specific paradoxical observations that will feel very comforting and will help you set up a healthy state of mind.

These paradoxes are true.

The only certainty is uncertainty.
Fear of death will stifle your engagement of life.
An acceptance of death will expand your appreciation of life.
The more you know, the more you know you don't know.
If something scares you, you should do it.

There is something profoundly powerful within this painful place you're in. How are you going to harness it and make what you are learning the most important narrative for yourself?

Reframing untold, unhelpful stories helps you calm your mind.

There are a multitude of 'What if?' stories in your mind.

Your imagination is conspiring with the rational part of your brain trying to 'solve' the cause of this terrible pain you are in. As if it is a reversible state. This 'secret rescue thinking' really stalls your ability to move forward. It is a dead end as there is no resolution.

Do you have an unhelpful story sabotaging your ability to move forward? People tell themselves these stories all the time. When a relationship ends with someone we love, we comb mercilessly over conversations and signs we didn't see.

When a diagnosis is made, we wonder whether being a vegetarian, or being more relaxed, or drinking less wine may have made a difference. As if we can control it all. This is a classic trauma response.

Below are some examples of unhelpful stories I concocted about Matt's death in my mind. I offer them to illustrate for you places you may have adopted irrational thinking for past problems that cannot be fixed.

CPR

In the Prologue I gave you a brief window into the day Matt died.

I believed that because I had failed to bring Matt back to life, I'd failed.

"If only I knew what I was doing. If only I tried harder."

I tried and I could not revive him. I had to accept the fact that it wasn't that I couldn't revive him - it was that he'd already passed. He had been dead for a while. It was an unrealistic expectation of myself in a very unhelpful story. Magical thinking at its most destructive.

This unfamiliar perspective drastically alleviated my guilt and shame. But I had to really challenge myself to see it.

"I didn't revive Matt. I couldn't save him."

He was already dead. Nothing could change that.

'I tried to resuscitate Matt, but he was already dead.'

What I know now? This is an excerpt from the Centre for Disease Control -

"Currently, about 9 in 10 people who have cardiac arrest outside the hospital die. But CPR can help improve those odds. If it is performed in the first few minutes of cardiac arrest, CPR can double or triple a person's chance of survival."

The Danger of Hindsight

Hindsight, with all the facts and the catastrophic events unfolding before us can serve as another way to punish ourselves for irrational reasons. As I stated before, we cannot go back in time. What is done cannot be undone.

Are there observations you have made since your loss that irrationally imagine you could have controlled the outcome?

When Matt was originally diagnosed, I was angry because I felt like I was being gaslit by both medical professionals and members of my family. During Matt's treatment, there were many moments where I was raising the alarm that there was a problem with the communication between the treating doctors.

Paperwork was disorganised and incomplete, and I could see that there was contempt and disdain in the relationship.

No one would listen to my concerns, and I was treated like a hysterical wife who didn't have a clue. I was furious about it. There was this outcome that could not be altered.

In hindsight I was working on the assumption that I had control over the situation and that I could have changed the outcome.

This created so much distress and anger for me. It was like watching a train crashing in slow motion as each poor decision piled up on the next until the sum of all the decisions proved fatal.

But I was not to blame. The professionals in charge of his treatment were to blame for poisoning him with the cardiotoxic drug. The arrogance of the specialists was to blame. The overburdened and under resourced system was to blame. The dysfunctional family I was in was to blame.

Think about all the 'if only' stories you have in your head. The spaces where you step in to become the director to get the story you would have preferred. There is no space for regret. The past really is the past. Let go of the idea that you could have changed the outcome. You are not to blame.

More Random 'B-Roll' Stories

I have this huge, big overarching narrative about my loss of Matt and my grief, but it's mostly made up of all these tiny little observations, and when I put them together there's always a moment when I can say,

"But that's another story," and it doesn't feel so big and consuming.

The Medivac Helicopter

We lived on a remote property up on the Hawkesbury River, so the emergency services sent a chopper when I called them. Knowing Matt, he would have loved to have been on that chopper. But he didn't get to go on the chopper because the ambulance had arrived, and they'd already pronounced him dead. They don't use choppers for body recovery. They only use them for transporting live patients in emergency treatment.

Premonition

I had a bad feeling that day. I didn't want to leave Matt. He wanted me to go to work because he had just been diagnosed and we were worried about money. He reassured me that he would be fine. We had plans to meet later in the day and travel to Sydney. Matt had generously donated (yet again) another sculpture to an art auction to raise money for Motor Neurone Disease sufferers to assist in their day to day lives.

It was such a strong premonition that I shouldn't be apart from him. As if the universe was tearing us apart. I think he had it too. Because the last thing that he ever said to me was,

"I love you more than you'll ever know."

Would my presence have altered the outcome? Or was the way it unfolded protecting me from seeing him die?

Telling Our Daughter

When I explained to Calpurnia that her dad had died, she howled. She howled in pain, and she said to me,

"Oh no. Like King Harold. Like Fiona's dad in Shrek."

Here was my little girl, having to use another story to understand what her story was because it was just so huge.

Dead Plants

Not long after Matt died, I ended up with a balcony full of dead plants. Everybody kept giving me plants. It felt like a test of my mental wellness. Whether I could care for them. Be in the small stuff.

I don't know if they thought that me watching flowers dying wasn't going to be a good thing for my mental health, but it was worse having the plants dying in front of me.

I could hardly care for my daughter and myself let alone care for the plants. I killed them all by overwatering, under-watering, overexposure, underexposure. They didn't stand a chance. Just another thing on my to do list that I was unable to do.

I felt so much shame about this. That I couldn't keep the plants alive. Now I've since figured out the limits of my care. And let go of responsibilities that are beyond me. I feel okay about saying no because I know my limitations. Be aware of your own too. I suggest, if anyone is foolhardy enough to give you anything that feels like too much to care for, regift it.

Hand Cream

When Matt died, people kept giving me tubes of hand cream. Fifteen different people gave me a tube of hand cream. I thought it was very odd. Was there some secret ritual to being a widow that I didn't know about that involved hand cream? Some subconscious Lady MacBeth inference that there was blood on my hands, and I was somehow responsible? To this day I can't wash that thought from my mind.

> "Out damn spot."

Not rational. I know. But see how easily we draw connections between unconnected things to make sense of sometimes random situations?

As you can see, there are as many stories as pebbles on the beach. Which ones are you going to pick up? And which ones do you let go? Just let them float away into the ether because they're not going to positively inform your life going forward.

It's tricky, because how you tell your stories affects your understanding of things. This is bound by your preconditioned ideas. About relationships. About childhood. About life.

But you are confronted with having no personal ideas about loss. Or grief. Or trauma. About recovering from a blindside. About what support looks or feels like because it is the great unspoken.

You may know what you're not getting. But have you drafted the story about what it is that you really want or need from the people around you?

You also have preconceived ideas about communication. About how you communicate and how other people communicate. Often, you work from assumptions that you communicate truthfully when there are layers of social code that prevent you from doing this. Sometimes it's extremely hard to ask for what you need.

And sometimes, if the reception is poor, silence is your best ally.

But we'll explore this in greater depth in Chapters 5 and 8.

In the end, all that is left of a person is stories. As you will be to someone else. Your misfortune has become a by-line in somebody else's description of you. But you are more than that. You are not your crisis.

Right now, you need to tell your story that will help you heal and find a way forward in your life.

Below are different narrative exercises for you to complete.

They are all about loss but relate to distinct kinds of loss. One is the loss of a person, whether through death, divorce, or estrangement. Another is the loss of a parent. The final one is processing the loss of self that can happen through illness.

Each are in letter form. Use the prompts as cues to set the specifics of the loss in your own life story.

Some clients do all of them. For parents, friends, or family they never grieved. Or a health issue they resent. A lover they said goodbye to.

Time to own your past, so you can claim your present.

What's your story going to be?

THE LOSS OF A PARTNER
The Beginning
When I first met you, I was...   years old.

We met at...

At the time I was living ...

At the time I was working...

My last relationship was with... and ended because...

When I first met you, I thought you were...

At the time I believed that love was...

When I look back at my younger self, I see...

When we met, you were...   years old.

You were living

You were working...

Your last relationship was with... and ended because...

When we met, you thought I was...

One of the first things I remember you said to me was...

What's Coming Up?
There will be conflicting emotions arising for you right now. This is normal. Highlight below what you are feeling.

SADNESS	ANGER	DISGUST	FEAR
ANTICIPATION	SURPRISE	TRUST	JOY

The Ending
When I lost you, I was...   years old.

You had been in my life for ...   years and...

At the time I was living...

At the time I was working...

When I lost you, I thought...

At the time I believed that love was

When I look back at myself on that day I see...

At the time you were ...   years old.

You were living...

You were working...

When I lost you, our relationship was...

The last thing you said to me was...

The last thing I said to you was...

What's Coming Up?

There will be conflicting emotions arising for you right now. This is normal. Highlight below what you are feeling.

| SADNESS | ANGER | DISGUST | FEAR |
| ANTICIPATION | SURPRISE | TRUST | JOY |

Letter to Your Lost Love

Dear _____

You're never going to read this. But it's important to me that I write it. The last time I saw you...

Now that you are gone, I ...

I want to tell you what it meant to share such a significant part of my life with you. In the time we were together, I learnt...

and I want to thank you for that.

Now that you've gone, I've learnt ...

The only people that know what goes on in a relationship are the two people that are in it.

When I think of our best times, I remember...

When I think of our hard times, I remember...

Since you've been gone,

What I miss most of all about you is ...

I always thought...

Now you are gone, I know you would want...

I hope you ...

Love,

What's Coming Up?

There will be conflicting emotions arising for you right now. This is normal. Highlight below what you are feeling.

SADNESS	ANGER	DISGUST	FEAR
ANTICIPATION	SURPRISE	TRUST	JOY

You will be feeling a little vulnerable at the completion of these exercises. It's important that you follow the self-care protocols as outlined in Before We Start (Pg. 22).

| BREATHE | EAT | HYDRATE | SLEEP | MINDFUL COMPANIONSHIP |

Releasing these trapped thoughts and feelings will initially feel uncomfortable. This is normal. When your feelings have come up, they will settle back in a new place, and you will feel lighter.

It is part of the process. When you have finished these exercises, rest. Let your subconscious recalibrate all the conscious intentions, memories, and recollections.

THE LOSS OF A PARENT

The Beginning

My earliest childhood memory of you is...

I loved it as a kid when...

When I was little, I thought that as a parent you...

My strongest childhood memory of you is...

I felt closest to you when...

When you supported my choices, I felt...

What's Coming Up?

There will be conflicting emotions arising for you right now. This is normal. Highlight below what you are feeling.

SADNESS	ANGER	DISGUST	FEAR
ANTICIPATION	SURPRISE	TRUST	JOY

The Ending

When I lost you, I was...   years old.

At the time I was living...

I was working ...

When I lost you, I thought...

At the time I believed that love was

When I look back at myself on that day, I see...

At the time you were ...   years old.

You were living...

You were working...

When I lost you, our relationship was...

The last thing you said to me was...

The last thing I said to you was...

What's Coming Up?

There will be conflicting emotions arising for you right now. This is normal. Highlight below what you are feeling.

SADNESS	ANGER	DISGUST	FEAR
ANTICIPATION	SURPRISE	TRUST	JOY

Letter to Your Parent

Dear _____

You're never going to read this. But it's important to me that I write it.

The last time I saw you...

Now that you are gone, I ...

I want to tell you what it meant to share such a significant part of my life with you. In the time we were together, I learnt... and I want to thank you for that.

Now that you've gone, I've learnt ...

The only people that know what goes on in a relationship are the two people that are in it.

When I think of our best times, I remember...

When I think of our hard times, I remember...

Since you've been gone,

What I miss most of all about you is ...

I always thought...

Now you are gone, I know you would want...

I hope you ...

Love,

What's Coming Up?

There will be conflicting emotions arising for you right now. This is normal. Highlight what you are feeling.

SADNESS	ANGER	DISGUST	FEAR
ANTICIPATION	SURPRISE	TRUST	JOY

You will be feeling a little vulnerable at the completion of these exercises. It's important that you follow the self-care protocols as outlined in Before We Start (Pg 22).

BREATHE	EAT	HYDRATE	SLEEP	MINDFUL COMPANIONSHIP

Releasing these trapped thoughts and feelings will initially feel uncomfortable. This is normal. When your feelings have come up, they will settle back in a new place, and you will feel lighter.

It is part of the process.

When you have finished these exercises, rest. Let your subconscious recalibrate all the conscious intentions, memories, and recollections.

THE LOSS OF YOUR HEALTH
THE STORY ABOUT YOUR HEALTH

My strongest childhood memory of somebody I knew being ill is…

When I was a child, I always felt … about my health.

When I was ill as a child, my caregivers would…

When I was younger, I always believed my health was…

Before I was diagnosed, I thought that health was,

The first time as an adult I experienced anyone close to me get very ill was…

When I received my diagnosis, I was…   years old.

At the time I was living…

At the time I was working …

When I was diagnosed and officially 'lost my health', I thought… about my health

At the time I believed that my illness was because…

When I look back at myself on that day, I see myself….

When I think of my future and my health, I imagine…

What's Coming Up?

There will be conflicting emotions arising for you right now. This is normal. Highlight below what you are feeling.

| SADNESS | ANGER | DISGUST | FEAR |
| ANTICIPATION | SURPRISE | TRUST | JOY |

You will be feeling a little vulnerable at the completion of these exercises. It's important that you follow the self-care protocols as outlined in Before We Start (Pg. 22).

| BREATHE | EAT | HYDRATE | SLEEP | MINDFUL COMPANIONSHIP |

Make sure that you have time on the other side of these exercises to relax and rest. You may feel quite tired or emotionally drained. Start your self-care by giving yourself this time to process.

Do you have food ready for the next meal? A quiet space to rest? Someone who can mind people or animals you may be responsible for? This is deep work designed to shift and release stuck feelings, so it will take far more energy than you might think.

Releasing these trapped thoughts and feelings will initially feel uncomfortable. This is normal. When your feelings have come up, they will settle back in a new place, and you will feel lighter.

It is part of the process.

When you have finished these exercises, rest. Let your subconscious recalibrate all the conscious intentions, memories, and recollections.

Remember to fill out your self-care diary this week to check your patterns of care and what kind of support you may need.

WEEK DATE:	MONDAY	TUESDAY	WEDNESDAY	THURSDAY	FRIDAY	SATURDAY	SUNDAY
BREATHE	YES x NO	YES x NO	YES x NO	YES x NO	YES x NO	YES x NO	YES x NO
EATING	OKAY NOT ENOUGH TOO MUCH	OKAY NOT ENOUGH TOO MUCH	OKAY NOT ENOUGH TOO MUCH	OKAY NOT ENOUGH TOO MUCH	OKAY NOT ENOUGH TOO MUCH	OKAY NOT ENOUGH TOO MUCH	OKAY NOT ENOUGH TOO MUCH
FLUIDS	OKAY NOT ENOUGH	OKAY NOT ENOUGH	OKAY NOT ENOUGH	OKAY NOT ENOUGH	OKAY NOT ENOUGH	OKAY NOT ENOUGH	OKAY NOT ENOUGH
SLEEP	OKAY NOT ENOUGH TOO MUCH	OKAY NOT ENOUGH TOO MUCH	OKAY NOT ENOUGH TOO MUCH	OKAY NOT ENOUGH TOO MUCH	OKAY NOT ENOUGH TOO MUCH	OKAY NOT ENOUGH TOO MUCH	OKAY NOT ENOUGH TOO MUCH
INTERACT	WHO? FELT GOOD FELT BAD	WHO? FELT GOOD FELT BAD	WHO? FELT GOOD FELT BAD	WHO? FELT GOOD FELT BAD	WHO? FELT GOOD FELT BAD	WHO? FELT GOOD FELT BAD	WHO? FELT GOOD FELT BAD

Three
Change, Choices, and Decisions

"When we are no longer able to change a situation, we are challenged to change ourselves."

Viktor Frankl 'Man's Search for Meaning'

Here is where we can start to build a relationship with the unforgiving. Life is continuing its formidable march forward.

It's easy to feel like you are being left behind.

You are at a new start point. Your days are punctuated by all these moments for which you're expected to feel grateful and part of something. People want to bring you into the fold thinking that you will feel better being sentimental in old rituals rather than uncertain in new ones. You can surrender those old rituals if they are too painful. You have my permission.

There's a commonly held belief that people shouldn't make any major decisions about their life for six to twelve months after suffering a big loss. This belief is founded in the idea that your decisions will be impulsive and detrimental to you. This is understandable as our cognitive processing skills don't work as well when we are distressed.

When we work with our emotions and distil meaning from our pain, we restore our ability to make good choices and decisions.

In Chapter One, The Crucible, we looked at how when we develop a relationship with our emotions, they are more manageable. In Chapter Two, The Birdseye, we looked at how perception shapes our emotional response and our meaning making. These are your emotions. They're your stories. And the steps you take going forward will be your choices. They're your decisions. It is your future.

Making decisions will create some momentum in your life. They will inject energy in this place where you are frozen in time. A decision does not have to be acted on in the moment. But the decision you make can generate another array of choices that you may be in a position to make.

Change creates uncertainty. The way to manage the uncertainty you face, is to start cultivating a relationship with trust. In this chapter, you are going to connect your emotions to the uncertainty of your situation and create space for them. When you can acknowledge your emotional responses, you will be able to trust your unknown future as your thinking will be clearer.

The relationship between emotions and change

> Change equals uncertainty.
> Uncertainty equals anxiety.
> Anxiety creates indecision.

Uncertainty can lead to a lot of distress. Not knowing what to do. Not knowing what is going to happen. Not knowing what other people are thinking.

Feeling uncertain can create anxiety for anyone whether they're grieving or not. This is because despite change being the only constant in our reality, we are not wired for easy adaptation.

Your Brain's Adaptive Skills

Our survival depends on our ability to detect errors in our environment and react quickly and instinctively. Our orbital cortex triggers the amygdala to draw energy away from the prefrontal cortex activating a surge of fear and anger. We need to escape the error or the pattern break.

Our brains run two distinct systems that inform our perceptions that dictate our responses to external stimuli.

The X System

The X system is reflexive. It is tuned into our immediate goals, past emotions, memory, habits, beliefs. It matches understanding and context with patterns on the fly. When you experience trauma and loss, the X system is confused by the data input as there is no pattern here to work on.

The C System

The C system is reflective. Its job is to constantly reflect on, challenge and correct the X system. It takes more energy to function and processes information more slowly than your X system. It takes things one step at a time.

When change is happening around us, we can feel threatened.

The motivation behind much of our behaviour is fuelled by our desire to minimise the threat and maximise the reward.

So, when you are in the throes of a trauma response it is normal to feel overwhelmed. It is physically challenging to think clearly. Your brain just wants to keep setting off the fire alarm.

More than one loss

When I reflect on my situation, my grief was not just at the loss of Matt, but it was the loss of our life together. It wasn't just his absence. His absence triggered a chain reaction of goodbyes to a way of life.

Saying goodbye to an assumed future that didn't exist anymore.

Where we lived. Who was around us. How we spent our time. Where we slept. What we ate. And all the shared tasks became mine alone.

I needed to grieve ALL the parts of my life I was saying goodbye to as everything changed. When a relationship ends, through death, or divorce, you're not saying goodbye to just one person.

It is the loss of you as you were in that relationship. That you is also gone.

When you experience ill health there are allowances that need to be made for treatment. Certain activities you can no longer undertake. A reduction in energy means that you will now have to evaluate who and what you want to spend your energy on.

So how do you deal with all the feelings that come up alongside this tsunami of change that is now your new life?

Let them come. Let the feelings be present. Name the feelings as they arise. Exercise your emotional literacy. Feel, feel, feel. Processing these feelings will create more clarity and reduce trauma spikes. And reducing trauma spikes will enhance your decision-making ability.

Often, we can become frozen in the sad ending because we don't want a new beginning. But our falling apart is also falling forward. Whether we like it or not, we are at a new beginning.

We can look at the past in our rear-view mirror, but we must face the future to see where we're heading. The future will catch you. You will fall and fall and fall apart but you will eventually hit a new reality. The world beyond the immediacy of loss.

Remember, the continuity has been broken. Not you. You are not broken. You need to regroup. You may have lost the person you would usually collaborate with. Your greatest resource. The one you would share your perspective with is no longer accessible. You may have lost a parent or friend who was a sounding board whose opinion you respected. You may have lost clarity in thinking due to illness and/or treatment. Energy to do the things you used to do.

The crisis of your loss will eclipse any opportunities to move forward until you become practiced at lowering your survival responses and naming and processing your emotions.

It will be hard to even see the opportunities while your amygdala is still sending you messages that you aren't safe. You need to turn that fire alarm off in your head. Breathing, hydration, rest, emotional processing, storytelling will all reduce the clanging so you can hear yourself think.

CHOICES AND DECISIONS

Choice is about selection, and decisions are about direction.

You may not feel like you can make decisions now. It is hard to find the energy to make decisions. It takes more effort to think about and do something new than to react out of instinct or out of habit. When we have suffered a loss and are caught in the uncertainty, we are yearning for the 'habit' of things. The uncertainty creates a risk aversion. That makes us less open to new things. We are less willing to explore or experiment.

And both exploring and experimenting are key to creative problem-solving. It's one of those life paradoxes that what we need to do, seems beyond our abilities when we are grieving.

And that's okay. What you can do is make choices that will make it easier for you to make decisions when you are ready. The decisions don't have to be acted on today. But making them will create momentum as you start working towards a possibility.

So how do you make good decisions while grieving? By making choices that will lead you to good decisions.

1. Define the principles you live by. These may be different now. Loss makes truly clear what matters to you.

2. Prioritise what matters to you. Put it before everyone else's expectations of you.

3. Play the long game. This is difficult, as it is hard to see too far ahead when you are grieving. Just the next step. Trusting that each right step will take you on the journey to where you need to be.

There are several factors that affect your ability to make choices and decisions. Each needs to be considered when you start looking at possibilities and opportunities. When it is clear to you how you are affected by each, you can then take steps to resist, resolve, process or rest.

FACTORS

1. Your emotions
2. Your energy levels
3. Your resources
4. Your familial and social influences.
5. Your level of satisfaction or dissatisfaction you hold with the current situation.

When you come to the limit of who and what you can be you are forced to change. And you will fundamentally change by virtue of the environment that you're in. And yet there is more than your environment at play. Despite what has happened to you. Regardless of how unexpected and crushing it is. There is a deep well of self to draw on. To dream and plan your way forward.

Make sure that you have time on the other side of these exercises to relax and rest. You may feel quite tired or emotionally drained. Start your self-care by giving yourself this time to process.

Do you have food ready for the next meal? A quiet space to rest? Someone who can mind people or animals you may be responsible for? This is deep work designed to shift and release stuck feelings, so it will take far more energy than you might think.

TRUST YOUR FUTURE EXERCISES

No matter the differences in our lives, we all only live in a day.

In that day you live somewhere. You live around others. You have things to do. You may have people you are responsible for. You may have duties and tasks you must complete. You are going to systematically connect your emotions to these factors and the uncertainty that surrounds them.

Go to your exercise book and answer each of the questions. Remember it isn't just about the living. It is about how you feel about it.

If you are struggling to name your emotions, go back to the pages with the descriptions in Chapter 1, Process. It's early days growing your emotional literacy, so refer to these whenever you are prompted for your feeling state.

Connecting Emotions to Uncertainty

Living Arrangements

How does your loss (partner, parent, or health) affect your living arrangements?

When you think about how your living arrangements are affected, what emotions are coming up for you? Try and name three.

For me it was fear, sadness and anger. Fear (anxiety) that I had to move and not knowing where we should go. Sadness (despair), that this way of life was ending, and anger (exasperation), that I'd only just moved and settled, and I was going to have to do it all over again.

What is the strongest emotion connected to the uncertainty of your future living arrangements? (For me it was the fear).

Social Environment

How has your social environment been affected by the loss?

When you think about how your social environment has been affected, what emotions are coming up? Try and name three.

For me it was sadness, anger and disgust. Sadness (grief), that I was so lonely and felt abandoned. Anger (resentment), that people put this invisible kind of shield between themselves and my pain, and disgust (repulsion), at the people who fed off the drama and behaved badly.

What is the strongest emotion connected to the uncertainty of your social environment? (For me it was disgust).

Your Purpose - What You Do

How has what you do been affected by the loss?

When you think about how your purpose/career has been affected, what emotions are coming up? Try and name three.

For me it was sadness, anger and fear. Sadness, (abandoned) because Matt and I worked together and were rarely apart. Anger, (frustration) because we had poured all the money we had made in the decade before into tools and growing his business. Fear, (anxiety) as I was going to have to figure out what I was going to do for us to survive and I had so little energy.

What is the strongest emotion connected to the uncertainty of your future purpose/career? (For me it was fear).

Who Are You Responsible For?

How is who you are responsible for affected?

When you think about who you are responsible for now, what emotions are coming up? Try and name three.

For me it was sadness (broken-heartedness), seeing our daughter grieving. Anger (annoyance), that people close to us weren't stepping up to help me support her, and fear (distress), as all the responsibilities were mine now.

What is the strongest emotion connected to the uncertainty of your future responsibilities? (For me it was fear).

What Are You Responsible For?

How does this loss affect what you are responsible for?

When you think about what you are now responsible for, what emotions are coming up? Try and name three.

For me it was surprise, as I was in shock at the scale of tasks I was responsible for. Anger, (frustration) as I was so overwhelmed. And fear, (worry) that I couldn't do any of it.

What is the strongest emotion connected to the uncertainty of your future responsibilities? (For me it was fear. The worry that I couldn't get through everything was exhausting).

Choices or Decisions

On the table make a note of what you can or want to do. Through this exercise you can start to build some certainty around what you do have control over. By exploring these possibilities, it will create trust in your future. You will feel better when equipped with the information that you need to guide you.

Considerations	No Change	Small Changes (Choices)	Decisions
Living Arrangements			
Social Environment			
Your Purpose (What You Do)			
Who You Are Responsible For			
What You Are Responsible For			

Remember to fill out your self-care diary this week to check your patterns of care and what kind of support you may need.

WEEK DATE:	MONDAY	TUESDAY	WEDNESDAY	THURSDAY	FRIDAY	SATURDAY	SUNDAY
BREATHE	YES x NO	YES x NO	YES x NO	YES x NO	YES x NO	YES x NO	YES x NO
EATING	OKAY NOT ENOUGH TOO MUCH	OKAY NOT ENOUGH TOO MUCH	OKAY NOT ENOUGH TOO MUCH	OKAY NOT ENOUGH TOO MUCH	OKAY NOT ENOUGH TOO MUCH	OKAY NOT ENOUGH TOO MUCH	OKAY NOT ENOUGH TOO MUCH
FLUIDS	OKAY NOT ENOUGH	OKAY NOT ENOUGH	OKAY NOT ENOUGH	OKAY NOT ENOUGH	OKAY NOT ENOUGH	OKAY NOT ENOUGH	OKAY NOT ENOUGH
SLEEP	OKAY NOT ENOUGH TOO MUCH	OKAY NOT ENOUGH TOO MUCH	OKAY NOT ENOUGH TOO MUCH	OKAY NOT ENOUGH TOO MUCH	OKAY NOT ENOUGH TOO MUCH	OKAY NOT ENOUGH TOO MUCH	OKAY NOT ENOUGH TOO MUCH
INTERACT	WHO? FELT GOOD FELT BAD	WHO? FELT GOOD FELT BAD	WHO? FELT GOOD FELT BAD	WHO? FELT GOOD FELT BAD	WHO? FELT GOOD FELT BAD	WHO? FELT GOOD FELT BAD	WHO? FELT GOOD FELT BAD

EVERYONE ELSE

Four
Your Emotional Software

Your emotional software is the unique program you're running on your 'system'. Our life experiences are all singular and unique, yet we all have similar parameters through which we experience life. And these are extremely broad.

1. That we are breathing.
2. That our five senses interpret our world for us.

Our eyes, our nose, our ears, our mouth, and the surface of our bodies collects all the information about our environment, that we then interpret. Even then, not everyone will experience life through five senses.

3. That we were born. That we age. And that we die.

That's all of us. Reduced to the experience of life as sentient beings. So, our 'hard drives' are the same.

What makes us all so specialised and unique is the software we are running. Some of these programs are biologically inherited. Most of the programs are decided by our environment. How do you feel about having your feelings? How do you feel about expressing them?

It's hard for anyone to predict how they will cope when they experience a life-changing event.

We all have an idea of who we are as a parent. Or a partner. Or a son or daughter. A sibling. A friend. And these ideas in a pre-loss world are mostly correct.

When things fall apart, it's unstable. There are two different scenarios that can unfold here.

1. You don't know how to express your feelings, and the people around you don't know how to respond to your feelings.

You can leave your feelings rumbling beneath the surface and everyone around you will constantly feel like they are on shaky ground because you don't understand what you are feeling and why you are feeling it. This will end in inevitable eruptions that may have irrevocable consequences for some relationships.

Or

2. You can start to explore how you feel about your feelings and this will help you develop your intuition about those people you are safe to express yourself around, and to flag those who are ill equipped for the depth of understanding and empathy that you need now.

When you figure out where you are with your own feelings you can start to navigate the relationships around you.

As we grow up, we learn to mimic our caregivers. At the time we don't even realise it. Our parents, our families, our communities set up the structure within which we relate to our feelings and ourselves. We are going to look back and release the shackles of the past to allow you to step into your emotional autonomy.

How does this relate to our feelings?

Our emotional programming develops in response to a varied set of influences that were imprinted on us all as children.

This imprinting created a secondary set of feelings that we all own, about having feelings. Simply described, they are 'the feelings about having feelings.' They are your meta-emotions.

Meta-Emotions

Just because we feel a feeling, it doesn't mean we understand it. Do you express your feelings, or seek support for yourself in ways that will help you to grow and mature? It is important to not feel distressed at your 'emotional inheritance'. Understanding it is the key to resolving it. Remember there's always room to upgrade to a better system and it won't require years of analysis. And once the upgrade is complete, there's no going back. Things will never feel the same again. Experiencing a challenging emotion will no longer just be about the event that has taken place. It is also now an opportunity to reflect on how easy or difficult it is to acknowledge and express that emotion.

The act of separating experience from influences creates a space to heal that programming if it is making it difficult. A chance to simply let go of what you may believe to be personal temperament but is honestly just inherited recycled experience.

Our meta emotional responses are social and cultural not primal. We don't just emote. We also respond to our emotions as we experience them. There are distinct factors that affect the emotional programs that we all inherit as babies and children.

These are: -

1. How our parents and caregivers responded to our emotional expression.

For example, a child is sad and cries. The caregiver responds negatively to the child expressing their sadness. This can be through minimising, indifference, or hostility. The social cue that is taught to the child is that it is not okay to express sadness.

How would you best support a child when they are sad?

I would acknowledge their sadness and comfort them. This would create a space where the child feels safe to share their vulnerability and be open to support. I can also do this for myself. **You can also do this for yourself.**

2. If parents or caregivers were able to understand, express and model their emotions in a healthy way.

For example, a parent is sad and upset at the loss of a relative. They try and hide their sadness from their children, despite the children being acutely aware of the parents' emotional barometer. (This awareness is how children survive). Sadness is modelled in a way that the child perceives it as shameful and that there is no one to share the burden.

Family

Growing up in the same house with the same parents does not mean that you have a shared emotional profile as other children that grew up in the same household. Many variables come into play.

1. The health of your parents' relationship during the first few years of your life.
2. Where you are in the birth order.
3. The demands of your siblings.
4. The attachment styles of your parents and siblings.
5. Your family's finances.
6. Whether there were health issues in your family either physical and mental, diagnosed, or undiagnosed.
7. Your gender identification and the emotional behaviours you were modelled by the same-sex parent as you.
8. The dynamics between your parents and you.
9. The dynamics between your brothers and sisters and you.
10. If you bore a resemblance to another relative physically or temperamentally.

The societies and cultures also affect the family expression you are modelled as you're growing up. This includes not just your family, but the country, the culture, the religion and where your childhood occurred on the timeline of history. We unknowingly inherit all this information that informs the systems within which we are living.

Society

Culture and religion will also affect the family system that you were raised in. You may no longer feel like you are part of that culture or practice that religion anymore, but you will still keep certain unconscious biases due to your conditioning. Following is a checklist of questions to respond to that will reveal some of the influences you may unknowingly still be affected by.

SOCIAL AND CULTURAL CHECKLIST

1. Did you grow up in a strict religious environment?
2. Did you grow up in a culture that discouraged emotional expression?
3. Was your country destabilised by war, civil unrest, or the aftermath of earlier wars? (There are few countries on this planet that can claim to be free of the inherited trauma of war. Even countries that see no action but send troops to fight live with the consequences of the military. Communities mourn the young men who did not come home. Or came home with PTSD and a difficult journey to return to 'regular' life ahead.)
4. Did you grow up in a culture where it was unsafe to express your thoughts or feelings?

We are all affected by meta-emotions. Everyone's meta-emotions are as unique and distinct as their histories and their life experiences. It is helpful to find the edges of your meta-emotions and those of the people around you. Being aware of this isn't an exercise in laying blame. It's not disloyal to reflect on relationships and their effect on you. This is part of your growth. Understanding all the pieces of the puzzle.

Everyone else you are encountering is also challenged by the complexity of what they are feeling in response to your grief, their own grief, and their own hardwired programming of how they regulate their emotions.

When you are grieving a loss, you are experiencing abandonment. You may feel that you were emotionally abandoned as a child. That you didn't develop a healthy relationship with your feelings and learn how to be with them. Perhaps you are now just realising that your own programming has left you under equipped to deal with being able to express your emotions. Even if your programming was reasonable, you are in fresh territory here.

Remember, our emotions are neither good nor bad. They just are. They may feel pleasant or unpleasant. But know that the sensation is temporary. They are our allies. Recognising them and responding to them will keep us safe.

Emotions and Time

You are experiencing all of these emotions in three different time zones. The past, with our memories and our life experiences. The present and how we're trying to function. The future and our anticipation of what's going to happen next. Although the origins of the feelings are in three different time zones, you're experiencing them all in the present. This is complicated. Exhausting. Muddy. We're going to find the placement of the emotion in time.

When you're remembering, you are in the past, but the feelings are happening in the present.

Emotions from the past require the action of healthy processing.

And when you are in the present, you are responding to your immediate reality.

Emotions in the present require the action of a considered response.

When you are preoccupied with the future it is still unknown and your feelings are projections based on your current thought patterns. This is where hyper-vigilance, fear, and anxiety dwell. It is also where anticipation and excitement live too.

Emotions about the future require the action of a measured projection and a degree of trust in the future.

Make sure that you have time on the other side of these exercises to relax and rest. You may feel quite tired or emotionally drained. Start your self-care by giving yourself this time to process.

Do you have food ready for the next meal? A quiet space to rest? Someone who can mind people or animals you may be responsible for? This is deep work designed to shift and release stuck feelings, so it will take far more energy than you might think.

How did you learn to regulate your emotions as a child?

Grab your notebook and reflect on each of these questions. Take your time. They are the emotional foundation of your expression today.

SADNESS

Did my parents console me when I was feeling sad?

Was it okay to feel sad?

Could I talk about feeling sad?

How do I feel about feeling sadness now?

Can I talk about feeling sad now?

ANGER

Did my parents care when I felt angry?

Was it okay to feel angry?

Could I talk about feeling angry?

How do I feel about feeling anger now?

Can I talk about feeling angry now?

DISGUST

Did my parents see me feeling disgusted?

Was it okay to feel disgusted?

Could I talk about feeling disgusted?

How do I feel about feeling disgusted now?

Can I talk about feeling disgusted now?

FEAR

Did my parents reassure me when I felt fearful?

Was it okay to feel fearful?

Could I talk about feeling fear?
How do I feel about feeling fear now?
Can I talk about feeling fear now?

ANTICIPATION

Did my parents listen to my plans?
Was it okay to feel anticipation?
Could I talk about feeling anticipation?
How do I feel about feeling anticipation now?
Can I talk about feeling anticipation now?

SURPRISE/SHOCK

Did my parents see my surprise/shock?
Was it okay to feel surprised/shocked?
Could I talk about feeling surprised/shocked?
How do I feel about feeling surprised/shocked now?
Can I talk about feeling surprised/shocked now?

TRUST

Did I learn to trust from my parents?
Was it okay to feel trust?
Could I talk about trusting?
How do I feel about feeling trust now?
Can I talk about feeling trust now?

JOY

Did my parents enjoy my joy?
Was it okay to feel joyful?
Could I talk about feeling joyful?
How do I feel about feeling joy now?
Can I talk about feeling joy now?

EVERYONE ELSE

Remember to fill out your self-care diary this week to check your patterns of care and what kind of support you may need.

WEEK DATE:	MONDAY	TUESDAY	WEDNESDAY	THURSDAY	FRIDAY	SATURDAY	SUNDAY
BREATHE	YES x NO	YES x NO	YES x NO	YES x NO	YES x NO	YES x NO	YES x NO
EATING	OKAY NOT ENOUGH TOO MUCH	OKAY NOT ENOUGH TOO MUCH	OKAY NOT ENOUGH TOO MUCH	OKAY NOT ENOUGH TOO MUCH	OKAY NOT ENOUGH TOO MUCH	OKAY NOT ENOUGH TOO MUCH	OKAY NOT ENOUGH TOO MUCH
FLUIDS	OKAY NOT ENOUGH	OKAY NOT ENOUGH	OKAY NOT ENOUGH	OKAY NOT ENOUGH	OKAY NOT ENOUGH	OKAY NOT ENOUGH	OKAY NOT ENOUGH
SLEEP	OKAY NOT ENOUGH TOO MUCH	OKAY NOT ENOUGH TOO MUCH	OKAY NOT ENOUGH TOO MUCH	OKAY NOT ENOUGH TOO MUCH	OKAY NOT ENOUGH TOO MUCH	OKAY NOT ENOUGH TOO MUCH	OKAY NOT ENOUGH TOO MUCH
INTERACT	WHO? FELT GOOD FELT BAD	WHO? FELT GOOD FELT BAD	WHO? FELT GOOD FELT BAD	WHO? FELT GOOD FELT BAD	WHO? FELT GOOD FELT BAD	WHO? FELT GOOD FELT BAD	WHO? FELT GOOD FELT BAD

Five
Manage the Moment

In this chapter, you are going to look at meaning mapping and the front line of communication. You are going to look at the stories behind the behaviour of the people around you.

We mourn as all mammals mourn. Mammals experience shock and distress when they are close to a death. When confronted with a fellow animal's body they pay respects and grieve. They understand the loss has consequences for everyone. Death rattles the very core of our existence. It is challenging to be confronted with our own inevitable demise at some time in the future. We can never escape death and we can never escape loss.

Grief is isolating for everyone involved. People don't know what to say. People don't know what to do. So often they say and do nothing. Because they believe it is safer than saying or doing the wrong thing but mostly, they are just reeling from the cold hard evidence of how fragile life is. Most people manage to tuck this uncomfortable idea away most of the time and focus on other things that we fill our days with. But often a person's actions are driven by a denial. A fear of death that can compromise their values and relationships.

A loss close by can reveal to people a level of dissatisfaction about their own lives they previously hadn't felt before. An urgency. People close can act out in unexpected ways.

They may start drinking too much. Perhaps taking drugs.

Some people experience a deep despair and futility in the life they are living. Some become very hostile and hide their fear behind anger. Some may take dangerous risks.

When people suffer a trauma, their prefrontal cortex doesn't work as well when the amygdala is driving. (Our flight, fright, freeze, fawn response.) Our prefrontal cortex is the part of our brain that is last to develop, and its job is to help us assess the consequences of actions we take. It is the control centre of risk analysis.

When people are traumatised, they may make unconsidered decisions that have long reaching and permanent consequences.

Like quitting a job. Or starting an affair. Perhaps separating from their loved one.

The ripple effect is real. And while your loss has affected you the most, there are consequences for everyone. People don't want to burden you with their troubles. You are already struggling. People do not know what to say or do.

The Single Outcast

If you have lost a partner, you no longer have an identity as part of a couple. Often people who have only known you as a couple struggle to redefine the relationship with you or, in situations where you are separating, decide that your ex-partner will be the continued friendship.

You no longer feel like part of the flock when a plot falls apart.

There is a repositioning that takes place. A recalibration of where you are in your world.

The Motherless or Fatherless Child

You have lost this very profound connection. The longest bonds since your conception have become severed. We may not all be parents, but we are all someone's child. The resonance of a lost parent is felt deeply. A seismic shift as we become the front-line generation. There is no buffer that separates us from our own ageing and inevitable death.

The Patient

In illness we cross a threshold to vulnerability. There is a 'before diagnosis' world, and an 'after diagnosis' world and nothing ever looks the same. There is a deep fear of dependence. A realisation that some plans and dreams need to be permanently set aside. At the very least, put on pause until treatment has finished.

There is so much grief in this space. There is this reflection that humans engage in that implies that our sickness is retribution. That we are personally responsible for our illness, and we have done something wrong. This is wrong thinking. So much of our culture denies illness and death. We turn away. And yet the only guarantee is that our bodies will suffer, and we will perish. It happens to everyone. Even the long-lived suffer the indignity of their bodies or minds betraying them eventually.

Language Around Loss

Our language also shifts to create context. We change lenses.

'The past the present and the future walked into a bar. It was tense.'

It is tense.
Before and after.
Then and now.
Past and present.
Future? Too hard.
Wife becomes widowed.
Husband becomes widower.
Child becomes orphaned.
Married becomes separated.
Separated becomes divorced.
Girlfriend becomes ex-girlfriend.
Boyfriend becomes ex-boyfriend.
Well becomes unwell.
Disease becomes remission.
Disease becomes terminal.
Employed becomes unemployed.

The present and the future have now become vastly different realities. And all reflections on that relationship are in the past while someone is in your life, they 'are'. When they are gone, they 'were'. It sounds so patently obvious and factual. Yet this shift in language is so difficult. Sometimes, the language people use around you just hurts.

The complication is that we mourn collectively but we grieve alone. Everyone around you has specific adaptations they're using to define your pain from theirs. To separate your despair from theirs. To support the illusion of control in their own lives.

When you experience a great loss, it is the randomness that leaves you bereft. That no matter what choices you believe you are making exercising your personal control, it can all come crashing down in the blink of an eye. You howl and cry and fall into a heap like a toddler. Unable to care for yourself, to eat, to drink, to wash. Closing your eyes in the hope that you will be rescued by a deep sleep and wishing that when you wake up, the loss was all a bad dream.

This falling apart is what sends people running from you. Your despair is just too much. These responses are not about you. It is not you.

It is the existential mortality shudder every person either consciously or subconsciously experiences.

Everyone else is asking themselves -

"What does non-existence mean to me?"

"What does losing love mean to me?"

"How can I avoid the pain I am witnessing?"

There are distinct behaviours that people adopt when responding to grief. Each of these descriptions will no doubt remind you instantly of someone you know.

Different Ways People Will Respond to You

Identifying

When a person responds to your loss by likening it to loss of their own.

When my mother died...
When my friend died...
When my brother died...
When my pet died...
When my husband left me...
When my wife died...
When (insert name here) was diagnosed...

Your pain is normalised. The message is: -

"You know this happened to me too."

You may end up consoling the person who is having these painful recollections from years and years ago. They are piggybacking personal history on your tragedy to process their unresolved grief and loss. It isn't intentional. Talking to you about loss provides them with an opportunity to express their own unprocessed emotions.

This interaction can leave you feeling like your own experience isn't important. The price of the companionship is denying your own immediate trauma. Sometimes it can be because a friend cannot differentiate between identification and support and sometimes it's a true reflection on the dynamic that has always been in the relationship. You did not see it before as you've never called on their support before.

How do we manage these conversations? By putting boundaries in place. You can do this by acknowledging their personal loss. A shared moment, but nothing more.

"I'm sorry that happened to you. It's difficult, isn't it?"

And if they don't read your cue,

"I'm really not strong enough to support you now."

It is okay to express how limited your energy is at the moment. If a person reacts with hostility, then it really is about them, and they've made that clear.

Denying

When a person initially responds to your loss in a familial, social, or culturally appropriate way then withdraws. They do what is expected in this situation, but they have no time to listen to you or witness you crying. This is an approach that tries to smooth over this tear in the fabric of continuity.

They ask you if you want to see a movie. Or check out a new restaurant. They'll send you gifs and kitten pictures on Facebook as if nothing has happened. They just want this to be a blip in the timeline and that you go back to being the person you were.

But you are not, and you never will be again. This is an attempt to control the effect of your loss on themselves. A dissociative cut off to prevent any seepage of pain into their well-managed life. It is a social connection that is conditional on your well-being.

Sometimes, sadly this can spell the end of a friendship.

It is not you. It is a behaviour. They have chosen to keep themselves safe. They are choosing to write themselves out of your story.

Philosophising

When a person falls back on truisms that dissociate from your immediate painful emotional response.

> "It's a mystery."
> "Life goes on."
> "Everything happens for a reason."
> "It was their time."
> "Time heals all wounds."

The idea that a well-ordered life with plans and hopes and dreams can just vaporise is terrifying. The consequences of your loss are unfathomable.

It's a kind of dissociation. People who adapt this method of communicating seem unaware that it isn't helpful. It can be infuriating. It is often used to avoid the discomfort of silence in emotionally distressing situations. Sometimes silence is what you need for processing.

Preaching/Proselytising

This response is when someone imposes their world view, faith, or belief system on you in your time of vulnerability. Usually regardless of any knowledge of what or whether you believe in anything.

> "I'll pray for you."
> "They are in a better place."
> "They'll always be with you."
> "God has a plan for you."

This is a behaviour people use that aligns with THEIR narrative. It is their chosen system and it's a comfort to them.

It's how they make sense of the world. But unless this is a spiritual bond that you have knowingly had and shared with someone, this behaviour is self-serving and inappropriate while you're grieving.

You might practice a religion but feel abandoned. In the face of adversity, your faith might be of little comfort to you. It isn't enough. This can happen.

Reminiscing

This response shuts down the trauma of your current emotional state by rapidly assigning your loved one's presence to the past.

> "He was…"
> "She was…"
> "Just last week I …"
> "Remember when…"
> "Do you remember the time…"
> "Where were we when…"

"It was only…"

Often you are not ready to let go yet. You are struggling so hard right now just to breathe sleep eat and figure out what comes next. Meandering down the cobblestone streets of memories is a luxury you can't afford, and it hurts. Not yet.

By prematurely shifting the discomfort of present pain into a sentimental memory bubble this person negates the rawness of the loss as you are experiencing it. Considering your trauma response is messing with your memory, it can be distressing to hear others recalling the past with such ease.

Ghosting

This is when a person responds to your loss by being there in the height of the drama and the funeral, or the split or diagnosis, then immediately afterwards withdraws.

"I've been so busy…"
"So much on…"
"I've been thinking about you a lot…"
"Wondering how you've been coping…"
"We must catch up…"

The person will check in on you once every couple of months to see how you are, but they don't engage in your new reality.

It is as if by occasionally checking in with you and finding out how you are, whether you're a mess or okay, it relieves them of their own guilt of having written you out of their everyday life.

There is a gap in the narrative. A space where people are recalibrating their connection to you. Can they cope with all the challenges you're faced with now? This added loss is further abandonment. It may be the price of expressing your pain. If so, that's okay. Create room in your life for the people that are willing to give you the energy and time you need. And if everyone walks? (This can happen with intensely traumatic deaths or diagnosis's), you need to create space to give yourself the energy and time you need.

You may feel very misunderstood and isolated right now but keep this in mind. Grievers are everywhere. The collective that is all the people in the world who share the grief of loss is endless in its breadth and scope. It is much larger than the network you're currently in. It is all sentient beings.

I have a running reminder with many of my clients. There are two kinds of people in the world. Those who have suffered heartbreaking tragedy. And those who haven't suffered heartbreaking tragedy. Yet.

Prepare to create room for the people who are ready to collaborate creatively with you. The people prepared to join forces with you as you re-imagine, rewrite, and transform the powerful pain of this loss into a different life going forward.

You have just stepped onto a larger stage in life. You are going to explore some strategies in the following worksheets that will alleviate your loneliness and help you communicate your needs to those close by that can support you. Despite your vulnerability you can set up safe boundaries to create emotional stability for yourself. You will do this by using scripts.

Scripts are extremely useful in high pressure situations. They allow space for you to disengage from the secondary injury or abandonment you may be feeling in the way someone is responding to your predicament.

The most reliable script is referring to your own truthful space of what it is you can manage. It's okay to admit you are overwhelmed by a conversation. You don't have to 'act normal' to make everyone else feel comfortable around you. That's for them to figure out. You can have a conversation about the communication.

RESPONDING TO THE RESPONSES

Identifying

When a person responds to your loss by likening it to a loss of their own.

Here are some examples of a script that may work.

"I can't talk about........ right now. Maybe at another time."

Example: "I can't talk about when your mother unexpectedly died in the hospital right now. Maybe another time."

Example: "I can't talk about when you broke up with Ian after your second child was born. Maybe another time."

In this way you are not negating their unprocessed grief, but you are creating a healthy boundary for yourself.

Denying

When a person responds to your loss in a familial, social, or culturally appropriate way, then withdraws. They then reconnect as if nothing has happened.

Openers.

"I'm really struggling right now. I'm just not ready to...

- see a movie...

- go out to a restaurant...

- attend a birthday...

- celebrate Christmas...for now."

"That's kind of you to think of me but I wouldn't feel comfortable...."

And if they insist: "No thanks."

And still insist: *"No."*

If it feels like pressure, realize the invite is to make them feel better, not you. I give you permission to NEVER feel obligated. NEVER. You always have the right to say no.

Philosophising

When a person falls back on truisms that dissociate from your immediate, painful emotional response.

"That's most likely true, but it doesn't make me feel better right now."

"It doesn't feel like that to me like that right now."

Preaching/ Proselytizing

When a person imposes their worldview, faith, or belief system on you in your time of vulnerability. Respond with caution. If people are emphatic, it is safer to withdraw than create a situation where their ideological comfort is threatened.

Responses -

"I understand that this gives you comfort, but it doesn't work the same way for me."

If you do have a faith system but it is no consolation for you at the moment-

"My loss is still so powerfully physical; I can't feel spiritual about it yet."

Reminiscing

When a person shuts down the trauma of your current emotional state by rapidly assigning your loved ones' presence to the past. This can bring up so many feelings at once and leave you very conflicted.

"I'm not ready to talk about this right now…"

"It's too soon for me to talk about memories…"

"It's hard for me to remember much now. I am still in shock."

Ghosting

When a person responds to your loss by being there in the height of the drama (the funeral, the split or the diagnosis) and then almost immediately withdraws. Don't try chasing this person. Let them go. Their behavior is telling you what they are equipped to deal with and it's not your pain right now. This behavior is complicated to decipher as it takes a while for the pattern to be obvious. There is just one metric to follow here. If you feel flat or sad after they have made contact, choose your moment. When it suits you. Let the call go to voicemail. Make an alternate arrangement via text to talk.

You take charge of when and how you are going to connect to relieve yourself of feeling abandoned. It's up to them. No contact is healthier than connections that leave you feeling marginalized.

Remember to fill out your self-care diary this week to check your patterns of care and what kind of support you may need.

WEEK DATE:	MONDAY	TUESDAY	WEDNESDAY	THURSDAY	FRIDAY	SATURDAY	SUNDAY
BREATHE	YES x NO	YES x NO	YES x NO	YES x NO	YES x NO	YES x NO	YES x NO
EATING	OKAY NOT ENOUGH TOO MUCH	OKAY NOT ENOUGH TOO MUCH	OKAY NOT ENOUGH TOO MUCH	OKAY NOT ENOUGH TOO MUCH	OKAY NOT ENOUGH TOO MUCH	OKAY NOT ENOUGH TOO MUCH	OKAY NOT ENOUGH TOO MUCH
FLUIDS	OKAY NOT ENOUGH	OKAY NOT ENOUGH	OKAY NOT ENOUGH	OKAY NOT ENOUGH	OKAY NOT ENOUGH	OKAY NOT ENOUGH	OKAY NOT ENOUGH
SLEEP	OKAY NOT ENOUGH TOO MUCH	OKAY NOT ENOUGH TOO MUCH	OKAY NOT ENOUGH TOO MUCH	OKAY NOT ENOUGH TOO MUCH	OKAY NOT ENOUGH TOO MUCH	OKAY NOT ENOUGH TOO MUCH	OKAY NOT ENOUGH TOO MUCH
INTERACT	WHO? FELT GOOD FELT BAD	WHO? FELT GOOD FELT BAD	WHO? FELT GOOD FELT BAD	WHO? FELT GOOD FELT BAD	WHO? FELT GOOD FELT BAD	WHO? FELT GOOD FELT BAD	WHO? FELT GOOD FELT BAD

Six
Choose Your Circle

"Destiny is what you are supposed to do in life.
Fate is what kicks you in the ass to make you do it."
Henry Miller

All this change is overwhelming. How are you going to manage the transition that life has presented you with?

Change is difficult in favourable conditions. But changes are easier if you initiate them in your life. When changes are forced upon you it's much more difficult to navigate them. You have been blindsided by fate and it has left you on the back foot.

Until now, your relationships may not have been challenged like this. How can you tell who is going to offer the support you need? You are in unchartered territory.

Other people perceive their connectedness to you using many different measures. Friends may think you have family support and distance themselves. You may have family support, but it's not the right support for you. Or it may appear that you have family support, but this may not be the case. Sadly, there are people who will further their own agenda at your expense. They will advertise their virtuous deeds to anyone who will listen. Brag about their imagined support that amounts to exercises in delusion and downright lies. I'm going to be uncomfortably blunt.

There are people around you who will use whatever adaptive behaviour has worked for them up until now. And you will discover whether their actions are based in self-interest or genuine concern. Picking the difference is the challenge ahead for you.

New friends may believe that your old friends are supporting you. And old friends may believe your new friends are supporting you and no one is supporting you. Some people aren't loyal to you. They are loyal to their need of you and once their needs change so does their loyalty. Many are too 'busy' for this pace of grief. They want to stay paddling on the surface of life. They like the superficial white noise that keeps any deep reflection at bay.

Sometimes it's not that people really change at all. It is that the mask falls off. Your relationship could only work provided the conditions in which it existed didn't change.

The Mnemonic for Grief

Get

Ready

It's

Everything

Freefall

Freefall is scary. It's also liberating. You have an opportunity to let go of the habitual relationships in your life that no longer serve you.

Last chapter, I described the identifier. These are the people who respond to your loss by likening it to a loss of their own. There is also a subgroup of these people who are deeply attached to their grief. It is the free pass they hold up to the world to excuse them of everything. They are the eternal victim. They will want to draw you into this place to come close to bond with you in your sorrow. There is truth to the old saying, "Misery loves company."

If you make your crisis your identity as they have chosen to do, they will reward you with their companionship. You may initially feel less alone. When you are grieving it can be hard to imagine that your immediate loss won't be the primary reality that defines you forever.

But watch what happens when you start taking the initiative. When you start taking responsibility for yourself. These people in the sorrow circle will become extremely uncomfortable. They want to stay in their problem-saturated story, and they want you to stay in yours.

And yet here you are, determined to help yourself. Taking responsibility and making choices. You are starting to understand how much you are truly capable of and you have changed. You are different. You may have been the person who others came to with their troubles. You may have been the wisecracking friend. Others may have always perceived you as stronger than them.

There are hundreds of stories people tell themselves. Most of them inspired by feelings they don't know how to process. The overriding one being that they don't know how to help you. They can't fix it or give you back what you lost. There is a deep despair. A suffering we know we all pass around like a hot potato. The dark night of the soul. One day it will be them. But not today. Today it's you. If you love, some day you will lose. If you live, someday you will become ill. It is a numbers game.

So how do you negotiate this? How do you manage these relationships while suffering the relentless daily reminders of your loss?

You structure your life in a way that you can stay connected to people who don't know how to help you. It is okay.

Even the people who let you down are part of the plan.

How? They disqualify themselves so another person better equipped to support you can help. They are helping you grow towards relationships that work at the depth you require.

Here are three steps to finding the right support.

1. **Accept that you are alone in your grief.**

No one will ever really understand what this loss means to you. There's an old Steve Martin movie called "The Lonely

Guy," where Steve plays this sad greeting card writer called Larry. In the scene where he walks into this fancy restaurant in his tuxedo and asks the maître de for a table for one. The lights go out in the place, and everyone stops talking. A spotlight is cast on him as he walks to the table. His aloneness is a social faux pas. He asks the maître de to take the light off him and for everyone to get back to talking. It's going to feel a lot like that at first. Accept it. It gives others permission to also.

2. **Accept that you are challenging for others to be around.**

Of course you are. People see in you what they want to avoid. Pain and suffering. Most people do not have the skills to provide you with the emotional support you need which leaves them feeling terribly inadequate and subconsciously angry at your predicament for highlighting their emotional incompetence.

All the conversations in the world ricochet with what others bring to it. They are punctuated with changing the subject, negating the reality, avoiding the bigger picture. You don't need an audience to process your grief. You need to commit to yourself 100%. Love yourself fiercely and fight for your future. How do you do this?

3. **Choose time alone.**

Don't sacrifice your well-being by keeping company with those who insist on you 'getting on with it'. Take time out to be alone every day. To wrestle with the feelings that come up for you. Work through these exercises. Journal about the sadness you are feeling. Take time to acknowledge and confirm the worries and concerns that you have. They are legitimate and deserve your attention.

4. **Let go of your expectations.**

Your expectations of others will only leave you disappointed.

If they could help you, they would help you. But as an unapologetically self-interested culture we just don't know how to show up. There are very few emotionally literate people. They are exceedingly rare.

5. **Be open to receive the practical support people can offer you while you are managing the effects of your grief.**

When you need help you have to look for it. At times it's necessary. There are people that are exceptionally good at a specific task. These people are specialists. You need to find these people and ask for their help. You are surrounded by people that can help you in the practical ways that you need. This will stop you from becoming stuck and overwhelmed in all your obligations.

Deferring to the right person's advice will ensure you are not anxious about whether you should make a decision and a change. There may be decisions you rarely make but they make often and acting on them will support you.

Every day your choices will start to affect your life. And in turn with practice each change will start to feel a little less threatening. Your physiological trauma response will start to abate.

HOW TO FIND YOUR CONFIDANTES FOR PRACTICAL SUPPORT WHILE GRIEVING

In chapter 3, we isolated all the distinct parts of your life that have changed. We reflected on the choices and changes that you are considering. We are going to revisit all those various parts of your life and see who can best support you at this time. Who are the people who can be your inner circle? It needn't be the same people for each situation. And you may be surprised at who turns out to be the allies you need. Keep your mind open.

BRAINSTORMING

Below are some prompts for you to think about what support you might need, and who may best provide it. Responding to them will shift your feelings about the future from anxiety to action.

Your Living Arrangements

Do you need to call your bank manager and talk to them about the conditions of your mortgage? What considerations need to be made if you've been widowed or you're separating?

If you are ill, do you have employment insurance? Can you draw on your superannuation? Can you get a support pension?

Do you have a friend who can help you find a good real estate agent if you're looking to sell or to move? Do you need to get a roommate to share the expenses if you are renting? Do you want to move? Is there a 'benevolent clause' that will help you in breaking a lease if you need to?

Your Social Environment.

Who are the people that can meet you where you are at?

Who is okay stepping into your environment to spend time?

Who doesn't care that your kitchen is a mess?

Who won't care if you cancel at the last minute or are still in your pyjamas at lunchtime or even dinnertime?

Your Purpose

Who are the big picture people you know? Consider people you know who have made big life changes and understand how challenging it is. They are looking down their reality tunnel and it's a unique perspective you may not have thought of. It may be just what you need.

Remember that people's advice is always a reflection of their subjective experiences. I think the quote is "Advice is recycled nostalgia."

It is not what they think of you. For example, if you've never worked an office job and never plan to then don't defer to the advice of someone who has only ever done this. Or if you value consistent job security then don't defer to the risk-taking artist whose income is sporadic.

And bear in mind the weight of family responsibilities may weigh more heavily on you now. Your previous way of working maybe isn't possible now. Or may require you to enlist additional household support. You may find yourself with all the childcare responsibilities. Or be juggling between custody orders or the boss that expects the same as it ever was.

If you're thinking of changing careers or going back to school and retraining, seek out someone who has done this. It doesn't have to be the same field of work, just someone who has had the experience of changing purposes and can offer you their insight.

Don't be afraid. You don't have to settle for half of a lost life.

You are starting a new story now. Who can inspire you, encourage you, and support you in this new chapter?

Who are you responsible for?

If you have children, they're grieving this loss too. At the most noticeable they're grieving that you are grieving. Who around you can take them for play dates and offer some normal in the complex state of things? Is there an after-school program they can attend to be around children to socialize?

Children are acutely aware of your sorrow and may be reluctant to approach you with their worries and troubles. Depending on their age, they may invent stories around the loss or illness. Try and give them age appropriate facts about everything. Then they won't have to invent stories to make sense of a situation they don't understand.

Is there a friend you trust to keep your child's confidence to support them? Is there a counsellor at the school you could meet with? A bereavement centre for children in your area? Is there someone you can think of that will be happy to research these resources for you? Find out what they can do to help you support your children. You can ask. The people who can help, want to help. They just don't know how.

And sometimes what children really need most is some space from your sadness.

What are you responsible for?

Is it tidying up? Boxing stuff up? Can you think of someone who can help you with this? Someone who likes to be organized. Who can get the boxes, the packing tape, the tape gun, the labels? Who can drop off things to Goodwill or the dry cleaners?

And if necessary, organize professional movers or some mates to help you if necessary?

You may need to do some financial planning. Can any of the people you know recommend a good financial planner to help you form a budget going forward? Or an accountant to help you with your tax return? If you are separating, taxes will be different as a single person. And if you're widowed it's true what they say about taxes and death. You will still have to file and pay your loved ones return and debt.

Are there government allowances you're entitled to now you're alone? Are there organizations that can help you?

Ask someone to research this for you and take you to appointments if you need to go. Some organizations and businesses require death certificates to shut down accounts. Get copies of the death certificate and ask a friend to have them notarised for you and follow up on contacting the relevant companies and getting them the information they need.

If you are having treatment for an illness, ask someone you trust to come and advocate for you on your behalf. It's helpful to have someone take notes while you are receiving important medical information. To get you there, and get you home and set you up with what you need.

People will want to help you in whatever small way they can.

They can't take your pain away, but they can help you with all these tasks that are so exhausting confusing and confronting while you are grieving. They want to be useful. And in some strange way by supplying a task for people to connect in a helpful way, it alleviates their fear of inadequacy around the heartbreaking stuff. It allows for the only kind of care and concern they may be capable of showing you.

To manage what's ahead of you, you need to become a manager.

Delegate. Allow others to race around and deal with government agencies and organizations. See if others can research information that will help you. This will create some space for you to process and grieve. To do the inner work.

It is difficult right now to see past the grief. It is all encompassing, like a heavy cloak. Developing insight into why people behave the way they do takes time, and it feels unfair that you must produce ways that they can support you in your challenges. They should know, right? They don't. They can't undo the pain of your isolation. They can only step into the darkness for limited periods of time. You are the only one in it 24/7. Everyone else's stability is no longer the reality you find yourself in.

Don't be shy about asking for help. Just be sure that you're asking the right person for the task at hand. Then you get what you need.

This is your journey. You are the pilot. Take control of what you can control.

This exercise is about applying the information you've generated brainstorming to find people who can help you to make the changes that you need to make. The second part of each circle exercise that highlights where people in your life are offering unsolicited or inappropriate advice is not about blame. It's about familiarity. Just because someone is close to the situation doesn't mean they have the full knowledge and abilities that you may need now.

This exercise is also about learning to trust yourself. That you are more than capable of taking the right steps to help yourself.

In Chapter 3, we looked at these distinct parts of our lives and explored how we felt about the changes ahead.

Your Living Environment

Your Social Environment

Your Purpose

Who You Are Responsible For

What You Are Responsible For

Naming the emotions and knowing that they are survival tools designed to protect you, made it easier to be with them. Voicing these hidden parts of you made them less crippling. Change seemed possible. Emotions connected to letting go of the way things were felt and processed. We are now going to look at the practical ways you can implement change.

YOUR LIVING ENVIRONMENT
PART 1

Who are the potential people that can help you? A bank manager if you have a mortgage to discuss options?

A real estate agent or a friend who is good at finding rentals if you need to move? A cleaner if you are unable to keep your space clean? A gardener/ handy person if you need someone to do the outside jobs? Refer back to the other questions in the brainstorm at the beginning of this chapter.

Remember to have no expectation. They don't need to know everything that's going on for you. They don't have to understand your pain. You need their help with the task at hand. Can they help with a change you are making?

Make a list in your exercise book and fill it up with the changes you want to make, and the people who can help with them. Add as much detail as you need. Names, phone numbers, websites, and recommendations.

PART 2

Is there a conflict between what is best for you and easiest for other people? It takes a lot of energy, time, and resources to adapt and respond to this new post loss world. Others may not have enough of these to help you. Perhaps your needs are inconvenient. They will want you to make choices that suit them.

These people are not your inner circle. If you can see what they are doing and don't stand up for yourself, it will cause resentment in the relationships later. It is perfectly okay to say no to other people's suggestions. They may not like it. But this is your life. You've got this. Even if you make choices that need to be altered in some way later, they are yours to make. Not anybody else's. This is your life.

Make a list of the people who are trying to control the process or outcome. Who is the person? What do they want from the situation? What is their motivation?

In your exercise book write these challenges out. It will help you place everyone in the right spot.

YOUR SOCIAL ENVIRONMENT
PART 1

Who are the people who are easy to be around? A coffee mate?

A mate who will quickly visit if you can't face the world?

A therapist or counsellor who is helping you? An online support group or forum for people in similar situations?

Remember to have no expectation. You may have to try a few different options before you find a social environment that suits. From the experience of myself and other clients, it was some time before going to a gig, or a gathering of a group of people doesn't feel terrifying. It's perfectly okay to retreat. One on one is often the best way to connect. Except of course for online where you might find yourself observing everyone else's posts before you decide to participate. You may decide that you don't want to participate at all. There is no one size fits all.

Make a list in your exercise book and fill it up with the changes you want to make, and the people who can help with them. Add as much detail as you need. Names, phone numbers, websites, and recommendations.

PART 2

Is there a conflict between what is best for you and easiest for other people? It is perfectly okay to say no to other peoples' suggestions. You aren't obligated to attend functions and events that will make you anxious. You don't have to 'group grieve' if you don't want to. They may not like it. But this is your life. You've got this. Sometime in the future you may feel like you are ready to do these things. It is up to you. Not anybody else.

Make a list of the people who are trying to control the process or outcome. Who is the person? What do they want from the situation? What is their motivation? In your exercise book write these challenges out. It will help you place everyone in the right spot. And remember, the way people are behaving towards you is about them. Not you.

YOUR PURPOSE
PART 1

Who are the potential people that can help you? An old mentor? A new one? Someone with a similar skill set? Another person you know that has also changed careers, or shifted work choices due to care obligations?

Maybe online support groups or forum for people in similar situations?

Remember to have no expectation. You may have to try a few different options before you find a work environment that suits. It is okay to try things and see what might work for you. There will always be limitations. There will also be unexpected opportunities that will arise too. Remember to trace your anxiety back to the source. The source is uncertainty. The action is to trust yourself. And trust the future.

Make a list in your exercise book and fill it up with the changes you want to make, and the people who can help with them. Add as much detail as you need. Names, phone numbers, websites, and recommendations.

PART 2

Is there a conflict between what is best for you and easiest for other people? Just because someone is offering you an opportunity doesn't mean you have to take it. If it doesn't align with you, say no. No one is 'doing you a favor'. If it wasn't beneficial for them, they wouldn't offer.

Make a list of the people who are trying to control the process or outcome. Who is the person? What do they want from the situation? What is their motivation? In your exercise book write these challenges out. It will help you place everyone in the right spot. And remember, the way people are behaving towards you is about them. Not you.

WHO YOU ARE RESPONSIBLE FOR
PART 1

Who are the potential people that can help you? A relative? A friend who has a solid connection to your children or surviving parent? School supports? Afterschool care programs? A babysitter? Are there any community programs like art classes or music classes for your children to attend? Can you find an online support group or forum for people in similar situations?

Remember to have no expectation. You may have to try a few different options before you find the right support. It is very difficult to fulfill all the tasks and obligations for vulnerable people in your care alongside the daily challenges of living with grief.

Often children need a lot of reassurance. If they have lost a parent, they are terrified of losing you too. If you have been diagnosed with a serious illness they will be thinking the worst. They may not want to let you out of their sight. This anxiety is a perfectly normal response. They are going to want to spend time with you, but also need to be apart to take a break from your grief and get separate support for theirs.

A surviving parent may also have other health issues and the level of support that they require is high. Avoid burnout by ensuring there is someone else who can share the load. You will need rest and downtime.

Make a list in your exercise book and fill it up with the changes you want to make, and the people who can help with them. Add as much detail as you need. Names, phone numbers, websites, and recommendations.

PART 2

Is there a conflict between what is best for you and easiest for other people? It's fine to thank people for their offer of assistance and decline it. They may not like it. You aren't obligated to accept crumbs just because you are in a tight corner. It is perfectly okay to say no to other people's suggestions. You aren't obligated to leave your children with a relative that isn't sensitive to their grief. You aren't obligated to accept help from someone that makes you or your children feel uncomfortable.

Trust your gut. Check in with your charges after they have been to any kind of program or visit with other kids etc. and see how it was for them. Did they feel safe? Did they enjoy it? Did other people take time to be with them? It is up to you. Not anybody else. This is your life. Remember. Your response. Your choice.

Make a list of the people who are trying to control the process or outcome. Who is the person? What do they want from the situation? What is their motivation? In your exercise book write these challenges out. It will help you place everyone in the right spot. And remember, the way people are behaving towards you is about them. Not you.

WHAT YOU ARE RESPONSIBLE FOR
PART 1

Who are the potential people that can help you? By 'what', I mean the 'stuff'. Anything not people related. Do you have a friend who you may feel comfortable with to help you sort through possessions that need to be donated? A contact who can sell items that you will no longer need or use on the internet?

Is there someone who is financially organised that can help you with sorting out a budget? You may need a solicitor for any legal matters. This is important if you have children that will need care. Are there community or government programs that you may be eligible for? Do you have a friend that can research this for you? Remember to have no expectation. You may have to try a few different options before you find the right support.

Do you need help navigating your medical insurance plans? Remember your thinking skills are compromised with the shock of it all and it's okay to reach out and ask for support. The paperwork is designed to be obtuse already. And certainly not designed to accommodate the mental state of a person navigating a new illness and what that means to them.

These processes are going to take some time. Removing and letting go of possessions can be quite triggering and traumatic. In my experience, it's best to box up the everyday stuff and put it in the garage or a space that you don't access often.

When Matt passed, I had an entire workshop of tools that needed to go to other tradespeople, or they were going to decay and be of little value. I put ads in the local buy/sell site and sold many of them. Others I offered to the local community organizations that would benefit. I hired a lawyer to assist with my will and an accountant to lodge Matts's final tax return.

Make a list in your exercise book and fill it up with the changes you want to make, and the people who can help with them. Add as much detail as you need. Names, phone numbers, websites, and recommendations. Get them out of your head and onto the page.

PART 2

Is there a conflict between what is best for you and easiest for other people? It is perfectly okay to say no to other people's suggestions. You aren't obligated to give people your loved one's possessions as mementos or gifts because they say so. It isn't open slather on their things, especially if they were jointly owned. People can be open to receiving mementos if you offer them, but any attempts to pressure you while you are traumatized, and grieving are unacceptable.

Say no. Just say no until you are ready to deal with these things. I have had a client whose family (in law) asked her to put all her late husband's possessions out in the courtyard and leave them to choose what they would like to take. People do crazy, selfish, and cruel things when they are in pain. Protect yourself.

If people insist on making unreasonable demands on you, it is perfectly okay to shut down communication. Leave them time to come to their senses. If possible, ask someone to act as an intermediary and approach them to back off.

So often, in grief, family relationships are tested and break down over meaningless sentimental objects because it is safer to be angry than sad. Anger divides us. Sadness reminds us of who we love and what matters to us.

Make a list of the people who are trying to control the process or outcome. Who is the person? What do they want from the situation? What is their motivation? In your exercise book write these challenges out. It will help you place everyone in the right spot. And remember, the way people are behaving towards you is about them. Not you.

Remember to fill out your self-care diary this week to check your patterns of care and what kind of support you may need.

WEEK DATE:	MONDAY	TUESDAY	WEDNESDAY	THURSDAY	FRIDAY	SATURDAY	SUNDAY
BREATHE	YES x NO	YES x NO	YES x NO	YES x NO	YES x NO	YES x NO	YES x NO
EATING	OKAY NOT ENOUGH TOO MUCH	OKAY NOT ENOUGH TOO MUCH	OKAY NOT ENOUGH TOO MUCH	OKAY NOT ENOUGH TOO MUCH	OKAY NOT ENOUGH TOO MUCH	OKAY NOT ENOUGH TOO MUCH	OKAY NOT ENOUGH TOO MUCH
FLUIDS	OKAY NOT ENOUGH	OKAY NOT ENOUGH	OKAY NOT ENOUGH	OKAY NOT ENOUGH	OKAY NOT ENOUGH	OKAY NOT ENOUGH	OKAY NOT ENOUGH
SLEEP	OKAY NOT ENOUGH TOO MUCH	OKAY NOT ENOUGH TOO MUCH	OKAY NOT ENOUGH TOO MUCH	OKAY NOT ENOUGH TOO MUCH	OKAY NOT ENOUGH TOO MUCH	OKAY NOT ENOUGH TOO MUCH	OKAY NOT ENOUGH TOO MUCH
INTERACT	WHO? FELT GOOD FELT BAD	WHO? FELT GOOD FELT BAD	WHO? FELT GOOD FELT BAD	WHO? FELT GOOD FELT BAD	WHO? FELT GOOD FELT BAD	WHO? FELT GOOD FELT BAD	WHO? FELT GOOD FELT BAD

CONNECTION

SEVEN
DIFFERENT KINDS OF EMPATHY

EMOTIONS RECAP

Chapters 1 and 4 mapped your internal emotional reality. The bubble of your unique and personal emotional experience. You did this by exploring your emotions and naming them. By connecting them to the felt sensation in your body, you began to understand them.

As you isolated each feeling, the compressed heaviness of heartache started to become less dense. Your emotional distress shifted to more manageable layers with stories attached to them. There are reasons why you feel the way you do, and they are perfectly valid.

Your emotions started to make sense. You could see the behavioural cue that the emotion is prompting in you to keep you safe. They are your compass in a world of confusion. Showing you the way. Keeping you alive.

What is your sadness telling you?

If you are feeling sadness, it is because you have lost an attachment that is significant to you. You feel abandoned and you feel sad. Your response is to grieve and cry.

The desire is to reattach to what you have lost. You want your balance back. This isn't always possible. Knowing this, you have developed techniques to self soothe. Continue to keep these practices up. They are significant tools in your emotional management kit.

What is your anger telling you?

If you are experiencing the emotion anger, it is because you have been confronted with an obstacle. The thought is that the obstacle is your enemy, generating the emotion anger. The response is to attack, and the function of anger is to destroy what's in your way. This isn't always possible. What is the story of your anger? It is separate from you.

What is your disgust telling you?

When you are feeling disgusted, it is because you have experienced something difficult to put up with or accept. The situation is toxic to you. You need to remove the poison to remain safe. Put your safety first.

What is your fear telling you?

If you are feeling fear, it is because you are threatened. You are in danger and your fear is telling you so. To stop being afraid, you need to escape what is making you afraid. Fear is a rational directive to keep you safe.

What is your anticipation telling you?

If you are experiencing the emotion anticipation (that can feel like anxiety also), it is because you are in unexplored territory. You need to map and gain knowledge of the fresh territory.

What is your shock (surprise) telling you?

If you are feeling shocked, it is because you have been blindsided by an unexpected event. The shock creates confusion. You need time to reorient yourself to this situation you weren't expecting.

What is your trust telling you?

If you are experiencing trust, you have made a meaningful connection. You feel safe and valued and want to groom and cultivate the connection. This way you can achieve and keep mutual support.

What is your joy telling you?

Joy is telling you that you are experiencing positive gains. That whatever is occurring is positive and beneficial to your life. We will always seek more joy. We cannot experience too much joy.

You also learned that feelings don't necessarily arise independently of each other. You can experience many feelings at the same time. And sometimes, they can be conflicting much like instruments in an off-key orchestra.

When we looked at your emotional software (meta-emotions), you learned about your influences. What informed the feelings you have about your feelings. At how you learned to regulate your emotions as a child.

It was helpful to reflect on the emotional programs you have inherited. It created a deeper understanding of yourself.

You learned that meta-emotions are social and cultural, not primal like your survival emotions. You don't just emote. You respond to your emotions according to your unique perspective. You explored how your meta-emotions are shaped in childhood by how your parents responded to your emotional expression. Their ability to understand and express their emotions affected yours.

You also learned that the familial expression you were modelled was influenced by the social and cultural systems it was embedded in.

This wasn't an exercise in laying blame. It wasn't disloyal to reflect on relationships and their effect on you. It helped you develop a deeper understanding of your emotional landscape.

By exploring this emotional landscape, you learned that everyone is affected by meta-emotions. Everyone's meta-emotions are as unique and distinct as their histories and their personal life experiences.

You also learned that your feelings are triggered by events in time. In your past, and your present and your future. Being conscious of the shifting between time zones can help in regulating your emotions. When you place your feelings in the right point in time, there is space for you to process. Every feeling in its place.

You now know that emotions from the past require processing. That is the action you can take.

Emotions about the present require a considered immediate response and that's an action you can take.

Emotions about the future require measured projection and that's another action that you can take.

Now you have enough data to focus on the interface of your inner and outer worlds and the best way to navigate them.

A person's ability to empathize with your predicament is limited by many distinct factors. The space where you interact with other people, the interface, requires solid personal boundaries.

There are three distinct kinds of empathy that people will show you. Affective empathy, cognitive empathy, and somatic empathy. Each of these have different subtypes.

AFFECTIVE (EMOTIONAL) EMPATHY

Affective empathy is the ability to respond emotionally to another person. This can be both positive and negative.

Positive Affective Empathy

This is empathic concern when a person displays sympathy and compassion for another person suffering. We all like to experience this. It feels comforting for someone to understand your emotional pain. You experience immediate relief when you are around this person. They 'get' it.

Negative Affective Empathy

This is when a person displays feelings of discomfort and anxiety in response to another person's suffering. They are distressed by your distress. This is uncomfortable. It can be hard to figure out who is soothing who and often it feels like a negative feedback loop.

The differences in a person's affective empathy response can be caused by a person's early childhood and developmental experience. As infants, we all experience personal distress. When we see the distress of others, by around age two, we start to respond in other oriented ways trying to help to comfort and to share.

The distinction between the two kinds of affective empathy could be due to how secure a person's attachment was to their primary caregiver. If an infant's needs were met, they were modelled how to soothe and comfort. If those needs weren't met, and they had an insecure attachment to their primary caregiver, they have no prior learning as to how to show and express proper affective empathy.

It's not personal when a friend can't comfort you without falling apart. They struggle with emotional empathy. The complexity of your situation simply overwhelms people that have not developed the emotional resilience to connect appropriately in distressing circumstances.

COGNITIVE (THINKING) EMPATHY

Cognitive empathy is understanding another person's perspective or mental state. It is distinct from affective empathy. That is because someone who strongly empathises emotionally is not necessarily understanding another person's mental state.

There are three distinct kinds of cognitive empathy.

Perspective Identification

This is when someone can relate to how you have been mentally affected by your loss. It is helpful when you can see that someone understands your current predicament. Your state of mind.

They can see the pressure you are under. They are aware that your mental processing has been affected and accommodate you. They feel solid and dependable.

Imaginative Identification

The second type of cognitive empathy is imaginative identification.

If a person has a wide comprehension of experience through books and movies and music and history, they have a broad mindset. They are in a powerful place to support you. Their scope of the lived human experience is wide, and they are open to engage with the possibilities of your 'future you' identity, not only this present blindsided you.

Strategic Identification

The third type of cognitive empathy is strategic empathy. This is the deliberate use of perspective-taking to achieve certain desired ends. Its application may sound very detached and business like, but it allows for support that is outcome focused. The sacrifice of short-term comfort for longer-term support is worth it. Be open to receive the value of this support.

SOMATIC EMPATHY

This is a physical reaction when you mirror your own responses to another's somatic nervous system. Somatic empathy is to feel in your body what another may be experiencing at a physical level. We are all different in how extreme our somatic responses are.

For example, we all have different thresholds to confronting imagery such as horror movies or violence. And so it is with grief. Some will feel its contagion and experience your trauma response physically and others may be immune to it. Somatic empathy can be difficult to be around. It all depends on how the individual is wired.

There are so many different variables that come into play when you are interacting with other people. And not all interactions are going to be comfortable or feel supportive.

How are you going to navigate the emotional energy of your personal interactions?

Using a simple boundary analysis method with the mnemonic CATS.

Caring

Anxious

Thoughtful

Shocked

'Cats' is a simple mnemonic device to keep your boundaries safe and stop the messy emotional bleeding that can happen around grief and loss.

Caring - Empathic Concern - Here is when a person displays sympathy and compassion for another persons' suffering.

Anxious - Personal Distress - Here is when a person displays self-centered feelings of discomfort and anxiety in response to another persons' suffering.

Thoughtful - Cognitive Empathy - Here is when a person understands another person's perspective or mental state.

Surprised - Somatic Empathy - When a person feels in their body what another person may be experiencing at the physical level.

You are going to connect specific personal exchanges with the responses and how they make you feel. By making the connections in your experience with the knowledge you now have, you are practicing a way to emotionally respond to any given social situation.

Under each of the headings, recall a response that you recognize from your personal experience.

Some of these recollections will feel uncomfortable and may make you feel upset. Let it come. Release the trapped pain of misunderstanding. It's not personal. Grieve the misunderstandings. Accept limitations. People can only meet you where they are at.

Caring - Empathic Concern - When a person displays sympathy and compassion for another persons' suffering.

1. I felt cared for when...
2. I felt cared for when...
3. I felt cared for when...
4. I felt cared for when...

Try and recall as many moments as you can where someone was extending themselves and was emotionally available and you felt safe. If you haven't experienced this, don't despair. You've got tools now.

Anxious - Personal Distress - When a person displays self-centered feelings of discomfort and anxiety in response to another persons' suffering.

1. I felt personal distress when...
2. I felt personal distress when...
3. I felt personal distress when...
4. I felt personal distress when...

Try and recall as many moments as you can where someone was behaving like this. Enough for you to have reflected on it later.

Thoughtful - Cognitive Empathy - When a person understands another person's perspective or mental state.

1. I felt understood when...
2. I felt understood when...
3. I felt understood when...
4. I felt understood when...

Try and recall as many moments as you can where someone was identifying with your practical problems. Not jumping in and trying to 'fix' them, but genuinely relating to the obstacles you are facing.

Shocked - Somatic Empathy - When a person feels in their body what another person may be experiencing at the physical level.

1. I felt shocked when...
2. I felt shocked when...
3. I felt shocked when...
4. I felt shocked when...

This exchange can leave you feeling completely overwhelmed. The person you are interacting with is bleeding their own unprocessed grief into your experience.

By profiling the different responses friends and family have to you, you will be able to choose your confidantes. In the early days of loss, our grief is unregulated and raw. Here is where we see the capacity of people to be alongside you. People reveal their strengths and limitations as support when they share their empathy style with you. It is not personal. All the different factors that you have explored that make up your emotional template, such as your literacy and your meta emotions, are also at play in their personal emotional template.

Remember to fill out your self-care diary this week to check your patterns of care and what kind of support you may need.

WEEK DATE:	MONDAY	TUESDAY	WEDNESDAY	THURSDAY	FRIDAY	SATURDAY	SUNDAY
BREATHE	YES x NO	YES x NO	YES x NO	YES x NO	YES x NO	YES x NO	YES x NO
EATING	OKAY NOT ENOUGH TOO MUCH	OKAY NOT ENOUGH TOO MUCH	OKAY NOT ENOUGH TOO MUCH	OKAY NOT ENOUGH TOO MUCH	OKAY NOT ENOUGH TOO MUCH	OKAY NOT ENOUGH TOO MUCH	OKAY NOT ENOUGH TOO MUCH
FLUIDS	OKAY NOT ENOUGH	OKAY NOT ENOUGH	OKAY NOT ENOUGH	OKAY NOT ENOUGH	OKAY NOT ENOUGH	OKAY NOT ENOUGH	OKAY NOT ENOUGH
SLEEP	OKAY NOT ENOUGH TOO MUCH	OKAY NOT ENOUGH TOO MUCH	OKAY NOT ENOUGH TOO MUCH	OKAY NOT ENOUGH TOO MUCH	OKAY NOT ENOUGH TOO MUCH	OKAY NOT ENOUGH TOO MUCH	OKAY NOT ENOUGH TOO MUCH
INTERACT	WHO? FELT GOOD FELT BAD	WHO? FELT GOOD FELT BAD	WHO? FELT GOOD FELT BAD	WHO? FELT GOOD FELT BAD	WHO? FELT GOOD FELT BAD	WHO? FELT GOOD FELT BAD	WHO? FELT GOOD FELT BAD

Eight
Degrees of Connection

STORIES RECAP

In Chapter 2, The Birdseye, you went back to basics and pinned down your unique perceptions around your loss. Doing this gave you time and space to settle into your private story.

Narrowing it down to this perspective allowed you to find some context in the chaos and confusion of the grief you are experiencing. You placed what you have lost in your personal timeline and recorded the facts of your blindside. You stretched your story to allow for the entire relationship to be explored and considered. With the person you have lost, or your health. With yourself as you were. You have reflected on the space across time for what you have lost to be recognised. Beyond this immediate grief.

By doing this you climbed up out of the valley of darkness to the mountaintop and could see the journey that led to this immediate point in time. It stilled the internal confusion. It quieted the chattering voices in your head of the trauma and loss that made your recall difficult. It silenced the voices that stopped you from creating coherence around your memories of your lost relationship. Or your health. You will always have those memories. You have not lost this part of you. It is yours forever.

Can you remember how it felt to record these moments? Just focusing on the raw emotional truths? What it was like to shift the moments from your head and heart and onto a page? To be brave enough to record the moments of despair and separation? To feel the sliding doors shut as you became separated from what you believed would be your life? To feel the gap of time between that moment and this moment right now?

By pinning this down, you were able to feel the continuity of your own life journey. Affirming your identity by expressing your unique perspective and your story is a necessary and powerful step. It may have been lost in your pain as you grieve.

You now know that you can always access this private story. You can keep it your sanctuary of understanding and know it was yours alone. It is yours alone to savour and treasure.

By stretching your story past the pain of loss, you are pushing your pathways to open and integrate the past into your present on your own terms.

You learned the value of knowing when to pause when the story feels too complicated.

"But that's another story" - is a helpful re-directive to calm both the racing thoughts and emotions that rise with recalling events.

It helps to not feel so overwhelmed. There are as many stories as pebbles on the beach. Which ones do you pick up? Only as many stories as won't weigh you down. As can fit in your pocket. You have got enough going on.

Remember that you are the editor too. And what do you leave on the cutting room floor? The B-Roll to look at later?

In Chapter 5 you explored how to manage the moment as the people around you use their personal narratives to connect. And you saw how language often fails us as we try to connect.

You learned that most people are just reeling from the cold hard evidence of how fragile life is. How things can change in the blink of an eye. And we manage to tuck this uncomfortable idea away most of the time and focus on the things we fill our days with.

You started to see the patterns of interaction for what they are.

That they are defence mechanisms that people use to keep themselves safe from your pain. When you discovered that everyone around you has specific adaptations that they are using to define your pain from theirs, to separate your despair from theirs to keep the illusion of control in their own lives, you learned how to manage the moment. You developed some artful strategies to deflect from your sorrow being compacted and cemented by other people. Specific turns of phrase to manage a moment of interaction can be applied.

By now, hopefully it has started to become second nature managing the moments and you are feeling less trauma spikes each day. You can navigate social situations a little more easily by deflecting thoughtless but well-intentioned narratives. This is lowering your social anxiety. Instead of not knowing what to expect, you have a good profile of exactly what to expect. You know how to get through it without being triggered. Chapter 2, The Birdseye, and Chapter 5, Managing the Moment have solidified your own unique perspective. You have claimed your personal narrative in the storm of stories around you and learned how to manage the interface.

When you are processing the emotions of a deep loss and transitioning into a different way of living, you need more depth of connections and less breadth of connections.

The degrees of connection are the varied ways that people present their narratives. They are not just face to face. In fact, most of our interactions occur using technology. And these different forms of technology have a hierarchy and social code all their own and it looks like this pyramid.

Face to Face

Video Chat

Voice Calls

Texting, DM's, Email

Social Media

Telegraphing

Degrees of Connection Pyramid

Degrees of Connection Pyramid

Face-to-face interaction

Face-to-face interactions are the most detailed and sensorily exact way to connect with another person. This is the platinum connection. Flesh and blood humans connecting in ways beyond words. Here we connect not only with language, but with all the nonverbal elements too.

Nonverbal communication refers to gestures, facial expressions, tone of voice, eye contact (or lack thereof), body language, posture, and other ways people can communicate without using language.

Video Chat

Video Chat applications such as FaceTime or Skype allow us to still connect face to face if it isn't always physically possible. This still allows for some nonverbal elements that enhance communication. You can still read each other's facial expressions, but you are in different places. Often in different time zones. It doesn't allow for physical connection like a hand on the back, or a hug.

Voice Calls

Voice Calls are still a high-value connection as we can glean a lot from the tone and delivery of another person's voice. The space of silences and the tone of voice enhance the connection beyond just the words alone.

Phone calls also have spontaneity. They are happening in real time. Some people don't like talking on the phone. Others do. It is a uniquely personal preference.

Texting, DMs (Direct Messaging), or Email

Direct Messaging. Texting, Direct Messaging and Email creates pauses in the interaction. There is considered calculation to the rapport rather than an instinctive response with verbal contact. Language without expression can easily be misunderstood. That is, the message intended is not always the message received. Email is a longer format than text and is usually used when there is more information to share than in a text. It is not a spontaneous exchange but one way like a letter. These formats are useful for specific information. They are not quality channels for any charged, emotional situation.

Facebook, Instagram, Twitter, Snapchat, TikTok

When social media started it was originally an online space where people who knew each other could connect. As it has evolved it has become a place where we can all find our tribes. You may have even found me on Twitter, Facebook, or Instagram. Across the web there are communities where strangers can share their experiences and build connections.

You may use some of these or all of these or none of these. The people you connect with may not be known to you IRL (In Real Life) but be cyber relationships you have cultivated only on the platform where you met.

These platforms can also be very public forums for private and painful situations. It can be emotionally triggering to scroll through others updates and feel like life is passing you by. Alternatively, you may find support unexpectedly from people you've never met who have experienced losses like yours.

Telegraphing

This is when someone contacts you to tell you someone else has contacted them to see how you are going. They want to know what's going on. How you are. But they are unable, for whatever reason, to connect with you directly.

The quality of your IRL (in real life) relationships will be altered by how people choose to interact with you knowing you are grieving. When and if people downgrade the channel of communication they're using to connect, they are signalling their inability to cope with the situation. This in turn should inform the depth of information that you are sharing with them.

People place themselves on the pyramid. They make a choice. It is not you. Nothing feels worse than receiving a text asking how you are that you respond to in a truthful way only to receive the response, "I can't chat now have a meeting."

Or,

"I'm just hopping in the car will check in later."

It feels like another abandonment.

And nothing feels better than when someone texts you and checks in when they can call you so you can have a long chat. Someone is setting aside time to connect with you.

People are busy. We all carry a lot of responsibilities. And we all use them as excuses to not step in and be there for each other. We have all done it. At some point in everyone's life they have avoided another who is in pain. It is instinctive to be afraid of pain.

Everyone struggles with the right channels of communication, and we can experience negative feelings when we get our timing, or our intentions mixed up. What you need to figure out is whether it is a mix-up or a rejection. Only then can you take steps to protect yourself from thoughtlessness.

You are going to take charge of these channels and allow less room for misunderstanding. You are going to control the channels of communication to protect yourself.

The old expression is 'a problem shared is a problem aired'.

It feels good to get a problem out of your head and articulate it. When it's spoken, the problem-solving part of your brain kicks in and starts working behind the scenes. But we need to be mindful of whether we are connecting to the right person in a suitable place and time to do it.

You don't want to post on Facebook your status and unwittingly start a stream of condolences from your high school mates who you haven't seen in years. That just feels awkward, hollow, and contrived. And watching the rolling feed of a friend's glamorous holiday with their beloved can feel painful and distressing.

Oversharing your feelings to people who respond with a distant degree of connection can also compromise your healing process.

This is your life. It is not a Facebook sideshow until the next drama hits the newsfeed. It's painful to have people lose interest and move on to the next stimulus producing story.

They don't know it is setting off these feelings in you. It's not deliberate. You weren't to know it was going to make you feel so bad either. So how do you censor the narratives you are bombarded with daily?

Systemise your methods of communication to ensure you are not blindsided, and by doing this take control of your emotional state. It doesn't need to be permanent and absolute. When you respond to the cues people are giving you, it can create space to have the conversations about their communication channel if you want to.

You will find that once you start expressing preferences as to how you relate to people, some will just fall away. All the connections you have, all the communication exchanges are ways people express their story. And by examining them, you can see what role they are prepared to play in being part of your life going forward.

Do they genuinely want to be a part of your life? What distance are they creating by the method of communication they choose?

You are at a critical point. By focusing on your story, on the shafts of light and possibilities that are breaking through the dense fog of your situation, you can choose support, or sufferance. The feeling that comes up when the phone rings or a text appears can be heavy, or it can be light. Trust this.

You are not bound to keep connections that don't work for you. It is okay to let go. You are at the start of a brand-new chapter.

At a place where you can integrate the past and what you've experienced and recalibrate your journey forward.

It is your story. You can only imagine the life you lost in the future. The path you didn't continue. The course you did not chart. Lift the anchor. Set your sails. You know what you are doing. What is your story going to be? And who is willing to witness your transformation?

CONTROL THE CHANNELS AND CHOOSE HOW YOU CONNECT

There are so many ways that people connect. Everyone chooses the method that is most comfortable or convenient for them. The methods vary in their ease, engagement and comfort for people involved. Some are useful for connecting with people far away.

Record each exchange you make and reflect on the primary method that someone uses. Initiate changing the channel of communication to a more comfortable one for you if possible.

For example, my friend Jill texts me. "How are you?" just as I'm walking into the supermarket.

A lot has gone on since we last spoke and I can't possibly type it in. I manage the channel of communication. I text her back. "Can we arrange a time to meet up or Facetime?"

She texts me back she's busy right now. I write her name in the Text column.

A family friend, Sam, calls my auntie who calls me to ask how I am. She calls me and tells me this. I write his name in the Telegraph column. I put my auntie in the Voice Call column.

My friend Nina is in NY. She texts me to organize a time we can Facetime. We only do it once a month, but it is so good to talk face-to-face despite the distance.

A friend from my past on Facebook, Leanne, posts a cryptic quote tagging me, to express her condolences over my loss. It unleashes a storm of questions about what's happened. From people who are not close enough to my current life to know my circumstance. I don't want people watching my tragedy from a distance. It feels invasive. I write her name in the social media column.

Carefully consider deactivating social media if you find it upsetting. You can reactivate it later if you choose to. Now is not the time to be interrupted on updates. You need to focus on you.

At the very least, deactivate notifications or remove social media from mobile devices and check in once a day or week if you must. This is going to feel uncomfortable. You are perhaps already feeling very isolated and disconnected from your environment. To start shutting down methods of communicating, shrinking your social circle appears as if it may reduce your social connections. It might.

But the quality of the engagements will be much richer and healthier for you. It is like a natural selection framework that will identify for you the people who are open to your unfurling and fragile new reality. The space where you will start feeling out the possibilities in front of you and fall forward.

By initiating a more fulfilling communication connection with people you are giving them choice. You can explain to them why you'd prefer a coffee than a phone call, or a voice call to a text.

Face-to-face	Video call	Voice call	Text/DM	Social Media	Telegraphing

Remember to fill out your self-care diary this week to check your patterns of care and what kind of support you may need.

WEEK DATE:	MONDAY	TUESDAY	WEDNESDAY	THURSDAY	FRIDAY	SATURDAY	SUNDAY
BREATHE	YES x NO	YES x NO	YES x NO	YES x NO	YES x NO	YES x NO	YES x NO
EATING	OKAY NOT ENOUGH TOO MUCH	OKAY NOT ENOUGH TOO MUCH	OKAY NOT ENOUGH TOO MUCH	OKAY NOT ENOUGH TOO MUCH	OKAY NOT ENOUGH TOO MUCH	OKAY NOT ENOUGH TOO MUCH	OKAY NOT ENOUGH TOO MUCH
FLUIDS	OKAY NOT ENOUGH	OKAY NOT ENOUGH	OKAY NOT ENOUGH	OKAY NOT ENOUGH	OKAY NOT ENOUGH	OKAY NOT ENOUGH	OKAY NOT ENOUGH
SLEEP	OKAY NOT ENOUGH TOO MUCH	OKAY NOT ENOUGH TOO MUCH	OKAY NOT ENOUGH TOO MUCH	OKAY NOT ENOUGH TOO MUCH	OKAY NOT ENOUGH TOO MUCH	OKAY NOT ENOUGH TOO MUCH	OKAY NOT ENOUGH TOO MUCH
INTERACT	WHO? FELT GOOD FELT BAD	WHO? FELT GOOD FELT BAD	WHO? FELT GOOD FELT BAD	WHO? FELT GOOD FELT BAD	WHO? FELT GOOD FELT BAD	WHO? FELT GOOD FELT BAD	WHO? FELT GOOD FELT BAD

Nine
Living Change and The Momentum Loop

CHANGE RECAP

You have learned that you are not wired for change. You are wired for homeostasis and for everything to stay the same. Our brains respond to patterns in our environment to stick to a course of action that preserves energy. If you have been safe before from doing what you are doing you should just keep on doing what you are doing. Our brains work through error detection on a threat and reward system.

Change equals uncertainty.
And uncertainty creates anxiety.
Anxiety creates indecision.

It is normal to suffer exhaustion at the very idea of all the changes you are facing. It is an uncomfortable biological state to be in when you're adapting to changes.

In Chapter 3, Trust Your Future, you looked at how to manage the external changes in your lived experience to navigate the functional way forward. I outlined all the different components that are your lived experience.

Your living arrangements
Your social environment
Your purpose and what it is you do
Who you are responsible for
What you are responsible for

You connected your emotions to the uncertainty you were feeling about the future and by naming the feelings they became more manageable.

Do you remember how it felt when you could express your sadness and realizing it is in your best interest to make changes? The fear you felt about making changes?

Knowing it was the uncertainty that was feeding your fear gave you a little more equilibrium in the circumstance. When you work with your emotions and distil meaning from your pain you restore your ability to be present and make good choices and decisions.

You also explored the difference between choices and decisions.

You figured out that choice is about selection. Making the best of a limited situation. Decisions are about direction. Choosing to create an entirely different situation because of a challenging one.

You learned how to make choices that will make it easier for you to make decisions. And the decisions do not have to be acted on today. By making choices and decisions you create momentum and start moving towards a possibility.

You learned that it was easier to cope with change if you define the principles you live by, and these may be different now. To prioritise what matters to you and play the long game.

You looked at the factors that affect choices and decisions.

- Your emotions
- Your energy
- Your limitations
- Your influences
- Your general level of satisfaction or dissatisfaction with the situation as it is.

Each needs to be considered when you start looking at possibilities and opportunities. When it is clear to you how you are affected by each, you can then take steps to resist, resolve, process or rest.

Change creates uncertainty and the way to manage uncertainty is to start cultivating a relationship with trust. To start to trust your future beyond the despair of loss.

In Chapter 6, you learned how to choose your circle. Other people perceive their connectedness to you using distinct kinds of measures and sometimes it's not that people change, it's the mask that falls off. Your relationship could only work if the conditions in which it existed didn't change. You have changed. You are different.

You may have been the person others came to with their troubles. You may have been the wisecracking friend.

Others may have always perceived you as stronger than them. Your expectations of others will only leave you disappointed.

If they could help you, they would help you but as a culture we just don't know how to show up. You learned that there are few emotionally literate people. They are exceedingly rare. You learned to be open to receive the practical support people can offer you when you are managing the effects of your grief. With all this change going on this is your journey and you are the pilot. You need to take control of what you can control.

Here in Chapter 9, Living Change you are going to address how to integrate these changes internally. You will apply the Momentum Loop as part of a process that will help you in keeping a balanced and measured perspective for the rest of your life going forward.

Over time you will become unshakable in your ability to manage this different reality.

You will know exactly how to manage your emotions as they arise. You will know exactly how to manage the stories you find yourself stuck in. And you will be fearless in change.

Understanding this internal process is the healthiest response to any untenable situation.

The Momentum Loop

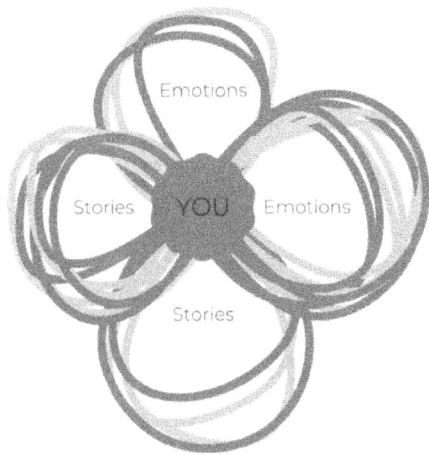

There are three steps in this process. All the knowledge and understanding you have gained in the modules is the foundation for each of these loops.

Here is the first loop -

Emotions and Stories

This is where we are connecting emotions and stories. You learned that your emotions are your survival compass, and they are telling you something important. You learned that your emotions always have stories.

I feel sad because...

Our emotions and stories cannot exist independently from each other. They are always linked. It is the stories you have told yourself that create the emotional response.

These stories can lead you down a spiral staircase to despair or help you cultivate balance by questioning the certainty of them being the only story.

Here is the second loop -

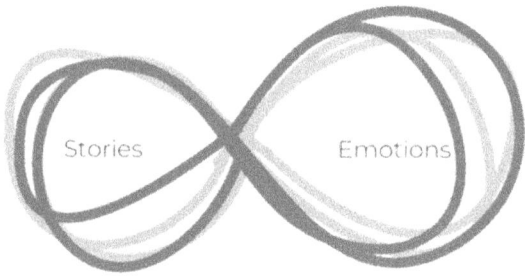

Stories and Emotions

This is where we are connecting stories and emotions. It is the reverse of the process in the first loop. When you receive information in a story, a version of events from someone else, or you tell yourself a version that lacks dimension or nuance, it can cause a negative emotional response.

Stories are how you make sense of your world. Your emotions are responses to stories.

"When this happened to me, I felt..."

"When I heard this, I felt..."

They cannot exist independently from each other. One may precede another, but they are always linked. There is no feeling without a story.

It is usually other people's stories that cause distressing emotions. They don't align with the way you make sense of the world. There is no story without a feeling.

The final part of the momentum loop process is putting it all together. Trusting ourselves and choosing to change our perception will ensure our emotional balance. You are the change. You alter the outcome of your lived experience by applying the momentum loop. By shifting gears. By shifting perception.

This is you, the eternal you, who was a baby being held, who smiled your first smile, who first noticed the wind in the trees, felt the sun on your face, felt raindrops fall on your head, falling asleep, who tastes flavors on your tongue, mammalian you, sensory you.

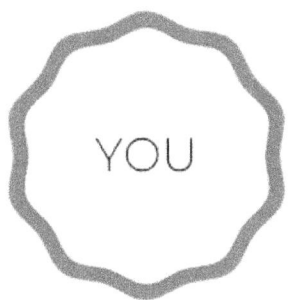

This is the edge of the eternal you where you connect with other sentient beings. Where you consciously create meaning with information from your environment.

This edge of you is where you must learn to keep yourself safe. It is where you experience understanding. It is where you experience misunderstanding. It is where you define your personal boundaries, and where your personal boundaries are crossed. Here, is where you experience your emotions and stories.

"My emotions are my survival compass. They're telling me something important. My emotions always have stories. Stories are how I make sense of my world. My emotions are responses to stories."

Working the Momentum Loop

When you are experiencing emotional distress, explore the story behind the emotion. Hop on the loop and ride into your meaning making, the story you have told yourself. The pain is woven into the expectation of a story that has more facets than you have explored.

Apply a new perspective. Every time we ask a question, we are generating another possible version of life because stories shape shift all the time. When other people's stories trigger a negative emotional response, you always have a choice. You can provide a counter-narrative or let it go, see their meaning making as separate from you.

The eternal you cannot be changed by another story. Only the edge of you can be affected, and you have the tools now to put the boundaries in place. With practice, this process will become second nature and you won't need to write out the factors to consider. You'll know when and how to check in and recalibrate your emotions and your stories.

BUILDING MOMENTUM WITH EMOTIONS
EXAMPLE 1

Emotion - I feel angry.

Story - Because other people keep comparing my loss to their loss, saying that I might have lost a partner, but they've lost a brother or a son as if I am being unreasonable about how losing Matt has affected me and that my response is too much.

The Eternal You - It is not up to me to console other people when I have nothing in the tank. I'm not obligated to submit to anyone else's hierarchical idea of loss. I will seek support from those who have the capacity to just witness and listen. It's not about competing narratives, just different ones.

The Resolution - I feel relieved that I'm no longer experiencing the ricochet of other people's unprocessed grief. Having boundaries protects me when I am vulnerable from being further hurt by others who are not considering the impact of their behavior.

EXAMPLE 2

Emotion - I feel afraid.

Story - Because I'm used to sharing the tasks that make up our family life and I'm not sure I'll be able to cope with it all. Everyone else seems to be so busy with their own lives and I don't want to impose on others. In my struggle to keep everything the same, I will let everyone down, including myself by expecting too much.

The Eternal You - Perhaps we are going to have to change up the way things are done. I'll need to prioritize what really matters for now. It is also not up to me to second guess whether others can or will help me. All I can do is ask, then I know where I stand.

The Resolution - I feel like I can better anticipate how we are going to move forward. By not sticking rigidly to trying to keep everything the same, I'm allowing a space for our family to slow down, to take our time healing and really think about what this new way of living is going to look like. I'm not having to second guess whether people will show up for me. I can ask. That's all. And if they can't help, well, they can't help.

BUILDING MOMENTUM WITH STORIES
EXAMPLE 1

Story - My friend just called me really excited to tell me that she had booked a vacation in the Summer, and she was really looking forward to going travelling and having a break with her partner.

Emotion - I feel heartbroken. I feel angry. I feel depressed and disappointed.

The Eternal You - It is perfectly normal that you would feel all of these feelings. Your partner who you loved to go on vacation with is gone, and you are being reminded how painful the reality is that you won't have this opportunity again.

The Resolution - My friend is not responsible for these feelings. My friend didn't tell me this to hurt me. She told me this to include me. And it hurts when I reflect on what I've lost. These are my unresolved feelings. I don't have the emotional bandwidth for other people's love stories yet. I am still in the 'twilight time' of recalibrating the past into the present.

EXAMPLE 2

Story - You're widowed now, and it will be impossible for you to ever get another mortgage so you must hold on to this house. It will be the only asset that you can confidently have. Don't make rash decisions.

Emotion - I feel trapped. I feel afraid.

The Eternal You - I know everything can change in the blink of an eye. I'm not sure that this financial security means much. Up until now I have been able to get by. I may need to ask for some help until I get a little more balance, but I'll be okay.

The Resolution - My value is being financially determined by my relationship status. I had financial security before I got married. Even before we bought a house. I don't want to hold on to this house and stay living here because this is as good as it will ever get. Matt died here. I tried to resuscitate him here in the living room. It is best for me and Cal to remove ourselves from the scene of the trauma. To find another space where we can start to build a different life and not stay in the remnants of the old one with all its associated sadness and pain.

As is evident from the examples, the stories are typically an external stimulus. A version of events or perception of the way things are, that triggers an uncomfortable emotional response. That emotional response is protecting you. It is guiding you. Trust it. Find your counter-narrative that aligns with your values and ethics and let the imposed narrative go. Trust yourself.

In your notebook follow the loop and practice this exercise. After a while you won't need to write the steps down. It is helpful at the beginning until it becomes an intuitive response each time you feel yourself pulled from the perfect balance of feeling emotionally centered.

Every time you are overwhelmed emotionally, come back to this simple exercise. Deconstruct the problem saturated story and take charge of how you are going to respond to the conditions of the world around you. It seems so easy. And yet it isn't. With each chapter you have built another layer of understanding. This scaffolding has allowed you to see yourself in ways that you hadn't considered.

When we learn a dance, we learn it step by step. When we learn a piece of music, we learn note by note. As it is with our emotional literacy and mastery. Step by step until it is intuitive, and you can trust each moment afresh as it unfolds.

I feel this because......

The emotion is...

CONNECTION

The story is...

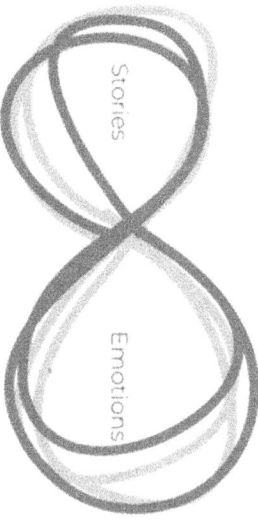

It makes me feel...

THE ETERNAL YOU...

- who was a baby being held...
- who smiled your first smile...
- who first noticed the wind in the trees...
- felt the sun on your face...
- felt raindrops fall on their head...
- falls asleep...
- tastes flavours on your tongue...
- mammalian you...
- sensory you...

THE EDGE OF THE ETERNAL YOU
THE RESOLUTION

- where you connect with other sentient beings
- where you consciously create meaning
- where you keep yourself safe
- where you experience understanding
- where you experience misunderstanding
- where you define our personal boundaries
- where your personal boundaries are crossed

Stories are how I make sense of my world.

My emotions are my survival compass.
They are telling me something important.

My emotions are responses to stories.

My emotions always have stories.

ABOUT GRIEF

Remember to fill out your self-care diary this week to check your patterns of care and what kind of support you may need.

WEEK NO: DATE:	MONDAY	TUESDAY	WEDNESDAY	THURSDAY	FRIDAY	SATURDAY	SUNDAY
BREATHE	YES x NO	YES x NO	YES x NO	YES x NO	YES x NO	YES x NO	YES x NO
EAT FLUIDS	OKAY NOT ENOUGH TOO MUCH	OKAY NOT ENOUGH TOO MUCH	OKAY NOT ENOUGH TOO MUCH	OKAY NOT ENOUGH TOO MUCH	OKAY NOT ENOUGH TOO MUCH	OKAY NOT ENOUGH TOO MUCH	OKAY NOT ENOUGH TOO MUCH
SLEEP	OKAY NOT ENOUGH TOO MUCH	OKAY NOT ENOUGH TOO MUCH	OKAY NOT ENOUGH TOO MUCH	OKAY NOT ENOUGH TOO MUCH	OKAY NOT ENOUGH TOO MUCH	OKAY NOT ENOUGH TOO MUCH	OKAY NOT ENOUGH TOO MUCH
INTERACT	WHO? FEEL OK? WHO? FEEL OK	WHO? FEEL OK? WHO? FEEL OK	WHO? FEEL OK? WHO? FEEL OK	WHO? FEEL OK? WHO? FEEL OK	WHO? FEEL OK? WHO? FEEL OK	WHO? FEEL OK? WHO? FEEL OK	WHO? FEEL OK? WHO? FEEL OK

Afterword

I am writing this just over eleven years since that fateful day when I lost Matthew. That moment where I reached a critical tipping point of true grief that completely untethered me. A lifetime of sorrows buried inside of me.

When adversity strikes, we are forced to grow. What we may have settled for is no longer acceptable if it is obstructing our growth. And we don't exist in isolation, but as members of families and communities and cultures that have their own hierarchical structures. If voicing and owning your own emotions and stories are perceived as acts of aggression, then the systems within which you have found yourself are awry.

You must choose what is right for you. You are not obligated to adopt other people's belief systems or advice about what your life should look like now. Self-care, understanding, and growth are not subversive activities. And the people around you that are threatened by your evolution? They are familiars of habit. Choose those that champion you, not defy you.

My journey as I was developing this process unearthed so many insights that could only become clear when my very survival was dependent on owning them. Trauma, porous boundaries, co-dependency, emotional illiteracy, and very little compassion for myself. Depression. Anxiety. A lot of self-pity. But no self-compassion.

My life is very different now. I attend to myself before any of my obligations. It is the only way I can be in the world honestly and kindly. Anger doesn't fester. I connect it to the story. I hold it up to the light. I challenge that story and develop more complexity to the narrative. This gives me the space and peace to respond. I am no longer afraid of my emotions as I understand their purpose. They keep me safe and true to myself.

Sadness doesn't lock in. When it arises with a random memory, or a photo, I let it come. And I can enjoy the happiness of that past moment remembered whilst lamenting its passing **at the same time.**

All is not lost. Everything passes, but all is not lost. Although we lose the person we once believed ourselves to be, this is what life is. A constant dying and rebirthing of our understanding.

When we can one day be grateful for our losses and the ways they challenge us to grow, it is then, and only then that we really know what it means to be alive.

Reading List

Abram, David. *The Spell of the Sensuous*, New York, Vintage Books 1997

Becker, Ernst. *The Denial of Death* London Souvenir Press, 1973

Bradshaw, John. *Healing The Shame That Binds You*, Deerfield Beach, Health Communications Inc. 1988 (Revised 2005)

Cameron, Julia. *The Artist's Way*, London, MacMillan, 1993

Campbell, Joseph. *A Joseph Campbell Companion: Reflections on the Art of Living*, New York, Harper Collins, 1991

Cashdan, Sheldon. *Object Relations Therapy, Using the Relationship* New York, WW Norton & Co. Inc. 1988

Chodron, Pema. *When Things Fall Apart*, Boston, Shambala Classics, 2010

Demasio, Antonio. *The Strange Order of Things*, New York, Pantheon Books, 2018

Erickson, Carlton K. *Addiction Essentials*, New York, WW Norton & Co. Inc. 2011

Forman, Mark D. *A Guide to Integral Psychotherapy*, Albany, SUNY Press, 2010

Frankl, Viktor E. *Man's Search for Meaning: The classic tribute to hope from the Holocaust*, London, Rider, 2008

Friel, John and Linda. *Adult Children, The Secrets of Dysfunctional Families*, Deerfield Park, Health Communications Inc, 2010

Hari, Johann. *Lost Connections. Why You're Depressed and How to Find Hope*, London, Bloomsbury Publishing, 2018

Heller L, and La Pierre, A. *Healing Developmental Trauma. How Early Trauma Affects Self-Regulation, Self-Image and the Capacity for Relationship*, Berkeley, North Atlantic Books, 2012

Hemingway, Annamaria. *Myths of the Afterlife, Images on an Eternal Reality*, Harts, O Books 2010

Jung, Carl. *Dreams*, New York, MJF Books, 1974

Jung, Carl. *Psychology and Western Religion*, New Jersey, Princeton University Press, 1984

Kornfield, Jack. *Bringing Home the Dharma, Awakening Right Where You Are*, Boston, Shambala Publications 2011

Krznaric, Roman. *Empathy, Why It Matters and How to Get It*, London, Rider Ebury, 2014

Levine, Peter A. *In An Unspoken Voice, How the Body Releases Trauma and Stores Goodness*, Berkeley, North Atlantic Books, 2010

Levine, Peter A. *Trauma and Memory, Brain and Body in A Search for The Living Past*, Berkeley, North Atlantic Books, 2015

Levine, Peter A. *Waking the Tiger, Healing Trauma*, Berkeley, North Atlantic Books, 1997

Lewis, CS, *A Grief Observed*, UK, Faber and Faber, 1961

Lewis, Thomas. Amini, Fari. Lannon, Richard, *A General Theory of Love*, New York, Vintage Books, 2001

Madanes, Cloé. *Strategic Family Therapy*, San Francisco, Jossey-Bass Inc.,1981

McGilchrist, Iain. *The Master and his Emissary, The Divided Brain and the Making of the Western World*, London, Yale University Press, 2010

Maltz, Maxwell. *Psycho-Cybernetics*, New York, Pocket Books Inc, 1966

Ornstein, Robert. Thompson, Richard. *The Amazing Brain*, Boston, Houghton Mifflin Company, 1984

Ornstein, Robert. *The Right Mind, Making Sense of the Hemispheres*, New York, Harcourt Brace and Company, 1997

Parrott, Les. *The Control Freak, Coping with Those Around You, Taming the One Within*, Wheaton, Illinois, Tyndall House Publishers, 2000

Perry, Bruce D. Szalavitz, Maia. *The Boy Who Was Raised as A Dog and Other Stories from A Child Psychiatrist's Notebook*, New York, Basic Books, 2008

Pollan, Michael. *How To Change Your Mind, The New Science of Psychedelics*, London, Allen Lane, 2018

Prochaska, James O. Norcross, John C. *Systems of Psychotherapy, A Transtheoretical Analysis*, Belmont, CA, Brooks/Cole, 2010

Rogers, Carl, R. *On Becoming a Person*, New Your, Houghton Mifflin Company, 1989

Slater, Lauren. *The Drugs That Changed Our Minds*, London, Simon & Schuster, 2018

Solomon, Andrew. *Far From the Tree, Parents, children and the search for identity*, New York, Simon & Schuster, 2012

Styron, William. *Darkness Visible, A Memoir of Madness*, New York, Vintage Books, 1992

Thanas, Katherine. *The Truth of This Life, Zen Teachings on Loving the World as It Is*, Boulder, Shambala Publications, 2018

Van Der Kolk, Bessel. *The Body Keeps the Score*, New York, Penguin Books, 2014

White, Michael. *Narrative Therapy Classics*, Adelaide, Dulwich Centre Publications, 2016

White, Michael. Epston, David. *Narrative Means to Therapeutic Ends*, New York, WW Norton and Co. Inc. 1990

Wilber, Ken. *No Boundary, Eastern and Western Approaches to Personal Growth*, Boston, Shambala Publications, 2001

Woolfolk, Robert L. *The Value of Psychotherapy, The Talking Cure in an Age of Clinical Science*, New York, The Guilford Press, 2015

Yalom, Irvin D. *The Gift of Therapy*, New York, Harper Collins, 2002

Yalom, Irvin D. *The Yalom Reader, Selections from the Work of a Master Therapist and Storyteller*, New York, Basic Books, 1998

Zimbardo, Philip. Boyd, John. *The Time Paradox, The New Psychology of Time*, London, Rider, 2008

Acknowledgments

I want to thank George Klein for holding the space in those early years when I thought I might just disappear. Those Saturday sessions sustained me more than you can possibly know George.

To my brother Simon Rowe and his wife, Kylie Rowe, who have been steadfast in the face of it all and supported Calpurnia and I in any way that they could. Your time, compassion and understanding have been a lifeline.

Thank you Tony Wilson, so generous with your time. Everyone needs to checkout the Speakola Podcast where Tony showcases the best speeches (famous and not so famous) in the world.

To all of Calpurnia's carers, who support me in filling Cal's life with joy and safety. Andre and Jessie Z you are absolute stars. And the people behind the scenes at GCCL who make it happen so I can rest easy that she's okay when I'm working. Thank you Leisa, Kirsty, Nicole, Nic, Cat, Jess and Christa for advocating so fiercely for my girl.

A huge thank you to my clients who have trusted me with their pain. Their courage as they show up to grapple with the big scary stuff is awe inspiring, and a powerful reminder to me on the daily that your response to loss is always a choice.

And lastly to my dad, Peter Rowe who instilled in me a passion for books, learning and creative solutions. He died in 2017 but would be absolutely chuffed that I wrote this book.

www.ingramcontent.com/pod-product-compliance
Lightning Source LLC
Chambersburg PA
CBHW051537010526
44107CB00064B/2761

9780645672800